THE INSIDER'S GUIDE TO STOCK CAR RACING

NASCAR RACING:
America's Fastest-Growing Sport

RICHARD HUFF

Bonus Books, Inc., Chicago

01   00   99   98   97   5   4   3   2   1

Library of Congress Cataloging-in-Publication Data

Huff, Richard M.
    The insider's guide to stock car racing : NASCAR racing, America's fastest-growing sport / Richard Huff.
        p.   cm.
    Includes bibliographical references (p.   ) and index.
    ISBN 1-56625-076-5 (alk. paper)
    1. Stock car racing—United States.   2. NASCAR (Association)
I. Title.
GV1029.9.S74H84   1997
796.72'0973—dc21   97-21393

Bonus Books, Inc.
160 East Illinois Street
Chicago, Illinois 60611

Cover photo and inside photos by Steve Colletti
Printed in the United States of America

To my wife, Michelle, and son, Ryan,
who have stood by me while I chased my dreams.

Contents

Acknowledgements		vii
Introduction		xi
1	**The Sport** — From Daytona Beach to Madison Avenue	1
2	**The Cars** — NASCAR's Steel Chariots	15
3	**The Drivers** — A Thirst for Victory	43
4	**The Teams** — The Men and Money Behind the Drivers	59
5	**Race Weekends** — Life at the Racetrack	79
6	**Pitstops** — High-Speed, High-Stakes Ballet	83
7	**Points** — Making the Grade	91
8	**The Sponsors** — Getting More Bang for Your Buck	95
9	**Television** — Bringing Racing to America's Living Room	109
10	**Safety** — Making Sure Everyone Gets Home	121
11	**Technology Transfer** — Racing for a Reason	133
12	**Tracks** — Stock Car Racing's Sports Palaces	139
13	**Travel** — Getting Around the NASCAR Circuit	157
14	**Team Addresses** — Making Contact with Your Favorites	165
15	**Publications** — Staying on Top of the News	173
16	**Racing Stocks** — Wall Street's Infatuation with Racing	179
17	**Statistics** — Stock Car Racing Milestones	181
18	**Glossary** — Words to Race by	197
	Index	205

Acknowledgements

This section of any book is very much like an acceptance speech at the Academy Awards. Though the actor gets the fancy statuette, there are usually a cast of supporting actors, directors, producers, managers, hairstylists who have in some way contributed to the winning actor's performance.

Books are no different. Getting to write about something you really care about at length is the equivalent of winning an Oscar. And like the winning actors, writers can't do it all by themselves. I'm no different.

There are numerous people who have in ways big and small helped this project come together. And like most actors, in my rush to get off the stage before the band starts playing the exit music, I'm likely to forget someone. To them, I offer my apology before I start.

So here goes.

I'd like to thank Tom Cotter and the folks at Cotter Communications, who have always been more than helpful in handling any questions I've had about the sport. Cotter Communications staffers Mike Mooney, David White and Mel Poole each went out of their way to set up interviews, sometimes with folks who were not clients of Cotter's respected firm. Also, thanks to former Cotter staffer John Singler, now at Garner & Nevins.

My gratitude to Drew Brown of Cohn & Wolfe, who handles public relations for Pennzoil-backed Bahari Racing, for setting up interviews and serving as a sounding board for my ideas.

Thanks to Paul Mecca who in this book and in my previous work has been a source of solid information and guidance. And to Goodyear's Carole Swartz for her help with interviews and figures on tires and technology.

My thanks to The Nashville Network's Charlie Munch and Nancy Neil, to World Sports Enterprises' Patti Wheeler, to NASCAR's Kevin Triplett, to TNN's Buddy Baker, to ESPN's Benny Parsons and Ned Jarrett, and to Ford's Greg Shea and John Valentine. Thanks to R.J. Reynolds' Chris Powell, whose weekly Winston Cup conference calls provided much needed information about the sport.

And to all of the folks who allowed me time to interview them for this or other works which have contributed in some way to the information contained within this book. They are: Bill Becker, Johnny Benson, Clyde Booth, Geoff Bodine, Thomas Floyd, Stu Grant, David Hall, Jeff Hammond, Doug Hewitt, Ronnie Hopkins, Jr., Dave Kenin, Chad Little, Larry McReynolds, Dayne Pierantoni, Ron Puryear, Tom Roberts, Felix Sabates, Bill Simpson, Robert Yates, Rusty Wallace and Darrell Waltrip.

A project like this also doesn't happen without the help, support and sacrifices of a family. No doubt, without their guidance this book couldn't have been done.

To my son, Ryan, thanks for allowing Daddy to spend hours working when we should be playing.

To my wife, Michelle, who while I was working on this book put up with piles of paper spread in virtually every room of the house, I offer my heartfelt thanks. She's offered constant support and has catered to my racing whims, despite any negative impact on her and our family. Somehow I'll make the hours up, of course, but not until after racing season.

Thanks to my mother for her continued support. And to friends Cathe and Glenn Slocum for constantly making me think I'm better than I really am.

My thanks to Steve Colletti a long-time friend and supporter who is responsible for the photographs in the book and on the cover.

Most of all I'd like to thank the folks at NASCAR, the executives at the company, the drivers, the team owners and the crew members for participating in a sport that gives so many people, including myself, so much enjoyment each week.

That music you're hearing is my cue to go. Again, my apologies to anyone I've forgotten.

Introduction

The setting was Accord Speedway, an upstate New York quarter-mile long dirt bull ring similar to hundreds of others dotting the United States. It was a summer Saturday night. We were there to watch a family friend — a local legend of sorts — race. I remember my first stock car race vividly.

Accord's aging stands were filled with fans, many just like us who had friends, neighbors and loved ones racing around the tiny speedway. I remember sitting in the bleachers that night, cheering on the men in their souped up cars as they zoomed down the track. I couldn't have been more than eight at the time. Before the first race of the night was over, I had fallen in love with the sounds, the smells, the excitement of stock car racing.

There's something alluring about a raceway. Though the drivers may be friends before the race, once they're on the track they become something larger than life. The fence separating the track from the fans also separates the men from the boys. Those on the track side are able to carry out what many of us have fantasized about many times before — driving a race car.

It has been more than 25 years since that first night at Accord. During that time my affection for the sport has grown only deeper. I'm not alone. During those 25 years the nation's appetite for stock car racing also has grown.

The boom is being led by NASCAR's Winston Cup Series, the premiere division of stock car racing in this country. Seemingly overnight the sport has moved out of the shadows and into the spotlight. In doing so, it has earned the well-deserved moniker as America's Hottest Sport.

Since 1990, attendance at Winston Cup events has nearly doubled and continues to grow. The number of people tuning in to live television coverage each year is soaring. Where television once ignored the sport, it's now a coveted programming option. Fans spinning the dial on weekends can find all sorts of motorsports programming from informational shows to actual race telecasts.

This book was written both for the new fans and those who have been following racing for a long time. In some ways it was born out of frustration. As a long-time fan of the sport and a newspaper reporter lucky enough to cover racing, I've often thought more could be done to inform the new fans about the very basics of the sport.

This book is designed to do just that. From the cars to the teams. From the sponsors to television. From the drivers to the points system. It's all here in simple terms. New fans will learn how cars are built while long-time followers are likely to learn something about how sponsorships work.

In putting the book together, I've tried to keep descriptions clear. If you're looking for precise diameters of the valve openings in a Winston Cup engine, you'll be disappointed. There are other books devoted specifically to engine building and engineering that should be consulted for those sorts of figures. Instead, here you'll find out what Winston Cup engine builders go through trying to squeeze out more horsepower so their drivers win on Sunday. You'll also find out how tires are developed for specific race tracks, how sponsors promote their products outside of the race car, and what life is like as a team member. I've also included a directory of team shop addresses which will come in handy when you want to drop your favorite driver a note.

There's a list of suggested newspapers, magazines and books that I highly recommend. I've been a long-time subscriber to many of them as well as an occasional contributing writer. They're all chock full of information.

Few people could have predicted the growth stock car racing has experienced in the past half century. And few can predict where it will stop.

Though I'm admittedly biased, I do believe that Winston Cup racing is the most exciting sport on the planet. It's part of Americana. The drivers have been described as gladiators and they are. Each week they go out and do battle, while at the same time risking their lives and careers. And it's one of the few sports left in which the participant's salary is based in part on his performance.

There's no way to truly understand the appeal of the sport until you've actually been to a race. It's easy to make snap judgements from watching something on television, but being at a raceway is a totally different experience. I guarantee, once you've gone you'll be hooked for life. I was and still am. I also believe that if you've read this book, you'll enjoy your trip just a little more, whether you're at Daytona or a first-timer taking in the sounds at Accord Speedway.

1

THE SPORT

From Daytona Beach to Madison Avenue

Imagine, if you will, sliding into a brightly painted stock car. Right leg first through the driver's side window and onto the seat. Rest your rear on the window frame and pull the other leg through. Now carefully guide your body through the opening and into the cockpit.

Once inside, you'll notice the grip of the seat. It's not fancy nor is it thickly padded like the comfy bucket seat in your Monte Carlo at home. The aluminum structure engulfs your body. A side panel cups the legs and curves inward to your ribcage.

Unlike the average passenger car, in this 3,400-lb. beast your legs are stretched out nearly straight. The steering wheel snaps into place on a column protruding through the dash board. The five-point safety harness, which a teammate has helped you fasten, is tight and unforgiving. There's no slack with the harness, it's there to hold you snug should you lose control and slam into a wall or worse, another car. You tug on the straps several times to prove to yourself that it is as tight as possible.

You reach for your helmet, which a team member has hung inside the car. A wild paint scheme has the sponsor's name splattered around the side. You reach back and hook up a fresh air blower to the side of your helmet. Radio wire connected to your ear phones. Gloves on. A small tube connected to a cooler filled with Gatorade is taped to the roll bar on your right.

Crew members scurry about on pit road. The vinyl cover over the windshield has been removed by one of your teammates. Another disconnects the oil tank heater from the side of the car. The oil in the 15-quart tank located behind your seat has been warmed so it flows smoothly through the powerplant in the front of the car.

As you settle in, a TV correspondent sticks a microphone into the car. You can hardly hear him through the helmet. And because you wear a full-faced helmet, he's got the microphone pushed into the eye opening.

"We're just hoping to have a good, safe race," you mutter.

You see the other team members stream by, grabbing onto any tools left in the car after it was pushed to pit road. They head to their respective pit stalls. The whirl of airguns fills the air. Quick bursts, machine-gun like. Nervous tension.

Some corporate executive, whose company no doubt has funnelled hundreds of thousands of dollars to the track owners as the race sponsor, ambles to a microphone. "Gentleman, start your engines."

The crew chief's voice crackles over the tiny earphones that have been formed to fit your ear. Crank it up, he tells you.

You reach over with your gloved left hand, turn on the battery switch and then flip the ignition. The 750 hp, 358-cubic inch engine under the hood roars to life. The rumble of the engine makes every piece of sheet metal on the car hum. You can feel it in your gut. Normal conversation with a passenger would be impossible. But there is no passenger. It's you against 40 drivers.

The gauges seem okay, water temperature, oil pressure, tachometer. No fuel gauge, you'll have to trust your crew for calculating mileage. A crew member helps you lift the window net, which is there to protect you from flying objects and from flying out of the car during a wreck.

There are no side-view mirrors, just a large rear-view mirror. Visibility, not a problem in street cars, is cut down dramatically by all of the roll bars and steel in place for safety. Roll bars are seemingly everywhere. Around you. In front of you. Above you. You sit in a protective cocoon, which you hope not to test — ever.

Letting off the clutch with the car in first gear you head down pit road. Unless you're on the pole, there are cars to the right or left and in front and behind you. Only a matter of feet separate one from the other. A NASCAR official, arms stretched out, guides you out of the pits. A crew from TNN stands at his feet.

Second gear by the end of pit road, third gear into the turn and fourth as you exit turn two. Slowly you guide the car off the apron and up onto the backstretch. Two-by-two the cars file through the turns and down the frontstretch. You're waiting for the green flag to drop. That'll mean the race is on. All bets are off. Friendships in the garages are left there. You're now gladiator heading out to do battle with 43 others mounted on their own steel chariots.

Several times during the warm up laps the crew radios instructions. The spotter, sitting high above the raceway, tells you to have a good race. During the event, the spotter will be an extra pair of eyes. If there's a wreck on the other side of the track, he'll tell you. If it's safe to move to the bottom of the track, he'll tell you that, too. For now, however, he's waiting for the starter to wave the green flag.

"Go, go, go," he says.

The flag is out and the cars come up to speed. Into turn one wide open, let off slightly into the turn and back on the gas midway through the turn. Stay low throughout, though when leaving the turn head to the outside wall. It's not hard, the G-forces on the car pull it toward the wall. Those same forces yank your body toward the passenger side of the car.

Flat out through the straight you reach speeds near 200 mph and head into the turn. Let off slightly, midway through ease back on and down the dog-leg front stretch. Aim for the infield and then the outside wall in turn one. Slowly off the gas and back on by the middle of the turn.

Now do that for 500 miles.

Sounds pretty easy, doesn't it? In reality it's anything but.

However, it's that very dream of being a race car driver that has helped make stock car racing the fastest growing professional sport of any kind in the country.

By all measures, NASCAR has experienced an unprecedented boost over the past few years. NASCAR has recorded attendance increases in each of the past 14 years and is not showing any signs of letting up. Sponsor interest is up. And television networks can't seem to get enough racing related programing.

From 1990 to 1994 attendance for NASCAR's premier Winston Cup series jumped 47 percent. During that same period, attendance for the National Hockey League was up 26 percent, IndyCar attendance was up 20 percent and the NBA's attendance was up 10 percent.

Long considered a sport enjoyed only by southern rednecks, stock car racing has become a fan favorite to people nationwide. The Winston Cup series has a season that extends from February through November and takes teams from New Hampshire to Florida, Michigan to Texas, California to New York.

This ain't your father's stock car series any more.

Indeed, the sport's new-found national appeal has attracted the attention of some of the largest companies in the world: Pepsi Cola, McDonald's, Budweiser, Miller Brewing, and Kellogg's just to name a few. Some 70 of *Forbes* magazine's list of the 500 top companies are involved in NASCAR racing on some level. No longer is NASCAR considered the exclusive playground for auto parts manufacturers.

The involvement of the major consumer products companies in racing has been one of the driving forces behind the growth of the sport. Now more than ever, consumers not aware of stock car racing are coming into contact with some reference during their everyday lives.

NASCAR is big business.

The foundation of today's stock car racing was laid in the late '40s by bootleggers in the South. During prohibition, moonshine runners used souped-up family sedans to outrun police who were trying to shut down their illegal liquor operations.

The bootleggers worked on their cars to make them faster than the police. They looked stock, but they were stock only in appearance. Bootleggers hollowed them out to make room for their cargo. And under the hood, the engines were tweaked to gain as much power as possible. In a drag race, bootleggers would win hands down.

Moonshiners bragged to each other about their liquor running exploits and the prowess of their hot rods. Eventually, an argument would ensue leading to a race. Those races evolved into Saturday afternoon events held on makeshift tracks in country fields around the South. Discussions of speed that started around a moonshine still were often settled on some farmer's vacant land.

Over time, races were set up by promoters, some legitimate and some not. In many cases, the promoters would collect what little ticket money there was from the fans and skip town before the race was over, leaving the drivers with nothing.

William Henry Getty France was born in Washington, DC, in 1909. He grew up a fan of racing and spent his formative years as a mechanic in the capital.

The young grease monkey would spend his free time at the local race tracks in the Washington-Baltimore area. He also raced his own homemade car at area dirt tracks.

France married Anne Bledsoe, a nurse whom he met one night at a dance. A few years later the couple had a son, William Clifton. Soon after, the France family packed up and moved south. The year was 1934 and France was just 25.

France stopped in Ormond Beach, Florida. As the story goes, the family sedan broke down, though he later admitted it was a minor repair he could have fixed in a day. However, France fell in love with the area, which included Daytona Beach and the Sir Malcolm Campbell beach-based speed show, and decided to stay.

In 1936, Campbell pulled up stakes and moved his show to the Bonneville Salt Flats.

Following Campbell's departure, Daytona Beach attempted to stage an automobile race on the beach as a way to lure tourists to the area. They created a track 3.2 miles long that would have the cars run one half a lap on the beach and the remainder on an adjacent highway.

The first race was a success from a fan's perspective, although for the drivers it was a mess. The beach turns got rutted fast, causing cars to flip over. The tide came in, taking a few other cars with it. And because one turn was completely blocked by the wreckage, promoters called the race at the 200 lap mark of a planned 250 lap race.

For the city, however, it was a money loser. So much so, town fathers wanted to bag the idea altogether.

But France stepped in and took over the promotion for the 1938 race and all following events. After several years of successful beach races, France expanded his racing series to a handful of tracks in the South and called it the National Championship Stock Car Circuit.

His own desire to better the sport, combined with tales of unscrupulous promoters, led France to believe that a unified sanctioning body was needed. He felt the crooks were giving racing a bad name. To fight the negative image, France wanted to create one strong organization.

He called a meeting of some of his racing friends from around the country in December 1947 at the Streamline Hotel in Daytona Beach. There he laid out a plan for the formation of a national organization to promote races. He wanted the rules to be equal for all. He also stressed that the cars had to be modern. Fans would want to watch brand new cars run, not old ones, he argued.

Before the meeting was over, France was named president of the organization, which would be named the National Association for Stock Car Automobile Racing. Soon track promoters from around the country joined the new group. NASCAR was incorporated in February 1948.

The first race under the NASCAR banner was held on February 15, 1948, on the beach in Daytona. Despite France's goal of having sleek new cars participate, NASCAR allowed drivers with old cars to race in the 1948 event.

NASCAR's first race in the new strictly stock or "new car" series — the forerunner of today's Winston Cup Series — was staged on June 19, 1949, at the Charlotte Speedway. Just as France explained at the Daytona Beach meeting, the cars had to race as they were on the showroom floor. Promoters offered a purse of $6,000, which previously was unheard of for such racing. The new car race, eventually called Grand National, was an immediate hit with fans. A year later, construction of the first superspeedway began in Darlington, S.C.

Darlington was proposed by race promoter Harold Brasington. In September 1950, Darlington held its first Southern 500, now one of the most prestigious and toughest races on the circuit. Some 25,000 fans turned out for the debut.

France liked the superspeedway concept and eventually built his own, the 2.5-mile Daytona International Speedway, which opened in 1959.

Under France's leadership, the sport of stock car racing started a steady climb. He ran the sanctioning body as a self-described "benevolent dictator." Had to be that way, he said. Democracy just wouldn't work. He made all of the important decisions and settled all disputes.

At times, however, he ruled with an iron fist. In 1950, when Curtis Turner and Tim Flock, two of his top drivers, tried to form a union, he suspended them for four years. Then in 1969 at the opening of Talladega drivers complained the track was unsafe. France jumped into a car and drove 176 mph to prove it was safe. Not convinced, the drivers walked off, led by Richard Petty. Instead of stopping the event, France filled the field with other drivers.

While maintaining the strictly stock credo, rules were altered to accommodate safety concerns and the increasing high speeds. Everything was done with an eye at creating a parity between the models. During some seasons, the number of NASCAR-sanctioned events for the Grand National series topped 60 in a 52 week stretch.

Thanks to France, drivers such as Petty, Fred Lorenzen, David Pearson, Cale Yarborough and Ned Jarrett became the stars of the series.

Auto manufacturers jumped into France's racing series head first. They fielded their own teams and funnelled large amounts of money into others. They saw the fan reaction and quickly realized that the sport could be used to sell cars. They lived and died by the saying, "Win on Sunday, Sell on Monday."

Despite their seemingly inseparable bond, NASCAR and the automakers didn't always get along. France's sole proprietorship troubled some and new rules occasionally drove them crazy. For example, in 1965, France forced Chrysler to run its Fury model instead of a smaller car that was lighter than the rest of the competition. Chrysler was furious over the loss of its powerful Hemi engine. Dropped out of racing, taking Petty, a shining NASCAR star with them. Petty sat out a year because of the dispute.

The relationship between NASCAR and the auto manufacturers changed in the 1970s, when NASCAR started getting a financial boost from an outside company — tobacco giant R.J. Reynolds.

Faced with bans on television commercials, Reynolds sought another way to promote its product. NASCAR proved to be the venue.

In 1971, NASCAR's Grand National division became the Winston Cup Series, named after Reynolds' cigarette brand. Reynolds used the sport to promote its product, but at the same time was promoting NASCAR.

Likewise, company's involvement in racing served as an incentive for other non-automotive corporations to jump into sponsorship positions within the sport.

In 1972, nearly a quarter of a century after NASCAR was incorporated, William France, Sr. turned the reins of the organization over to his son, William France, Jr. France, Sr. died in 1992.

The sport continued to grow and prosper under France, Jr. New sponsors infiltrated the sport and the fan base grew. He also maintained the benevolent dictator status of his father, making and reversing decisions where necessary.

Stock car racing got its biggest boost in the mid-1980s when an upstart cable network called ESPN decided to make it a programming staple. Before ESPN, television coverage of racing was limited to the annual coverage of the Daytona 500 on CBS and a few sporadic pre-taped telecasts during the season.

Live coverage of the races on a regular basis worked like a proverbial light switch for the sport. Viewers who never had seen a stock car race could watch from home in the comfort of their Barcalounger. Sponsors noticed, too. By putting their names on the sides of cars, companies found they got two bangs for their buck: at the speedway and at home.

Sponsors also found that fans were extremely loyal to the drivers, and, more important, to the products promoted on the sides of the race cars.

Drivers such as Petty, Yarborough, Darrell Waltrip, Dale Earnhardt and Harry Gant, went from being big stars in the South only to being household names everywhere.

Track owners also benefited from television. Shortly after each televised race, track owners would see the demand for tickets soar as fans wanted to get a taste of the speed and thunder up close.

That trend continues today. Some 5.6 million fans took in one of the 31 Winston Cup races on the 1996 schedule, up 4.9 percent from the year before. Millions more watched at home on TV. In 1979, only one race aired live each season. Today, every Winston Cup event and its companion event airs live. Weekends are filled with motorsports and Winston Cup programs feeding what is now an insatiable appetite for information about the sport. More such shows are on the way.

Since television began airing NASCAR events, the sport has taken off like a rocket. In the nearly 50 years since NASCAR was founded, the sanctioning body itself has grown into a $2 billion a year operation, according to *Forbes* magazine. That does not take into account the amount of money being spent or earned by the teams, the sponsors or the ancillary businesses.

Since 1949, NASCAR has sanctioned nearly 1,800 events for what is the Winston Cup circuit and paid out almost $350 million in prize money.

It's not only the drivers who generate sizable revenues from the sport. Stock car racing has become a significant business for all involved. The television networks carrying races are generating millions in additional advertising revenues from the sport. Sales of collectibles and souvenirs is nearly $800 million a year and growing. Just five years earlier, NASCAR collectibles accounted for only $60 million in sales.

And, each area staging a Winston Cup race benefits by direct and indirect expenditures from race fans and teams.

Before the 1997 season, North Carolina Congressman Robert Brawley estimated that racing brought an estimated $1 billion to the state's economy every year. Penske Motorsports, which built the California Speedway, estimates that the track will have an economic impact on the surrounding area of $125 million a year. And in 1995, fans attending the two annual races held at Dover Downs International Speedway put about $38 million of new revenue into the region.

The boom in Winston Cup racing is being pushed by two forces in addition to television: NASCAR and the sponsors. The sponsors have generated the greatest increase in interest. Every year, new non-automotive companies step into the sponsorship field. As a result, they're spreading the word about racing to a new audience. Walk through a supermarket nowadays and you'll find a dozen products ranging from cereal to Eggo waffles to laundry detergent bearing the likeness of a Winston Cup driver or his car.

The sponsors realized early that the best way to support their on-track efforts was to promote their products and their connection to the sport away from the raceway. The result, however, has been to boost interest in the sport as a whole.

Sponsors have also taken to using NASCAR as a way to foster new business relationships and to entertain their customer base, taking the place of skyboxes at basketball and hockey arenas around the country. With that, they've lured a more upscale clientele to racing.

NASCAR only recently has taken a hard stance in marketing itself beyond the traditional racing marketplace. Now there are NASCAR merchandise stores, not unlike Disney or Warner Bros. outlets, and NASCAR Cafes to rival the Hard Rock Cafes and Planet Hollywoods of the world. NASCAR has also increased its share of the licensing business, which until just a few years ago was handled almost exclusively by the drivers and the teams. Now NASCAR is aggressively approaching the licensing market, finding new products and companies to link with.

NASCAR has also been wise in expanding the sites of its scheduled events beyond the South to the Northeast, the Midwest and the west coast. It's truly a national sport to be considered in the same terms as football, basketball, baseball and hockey.

Today, 1995 champ Jeff Gordon is a household name, making occasional appearances on CBS' "Late Show with David Letterman" and being featured in an ongoing campaign for milk products. If Richard Petty is the face of NASCAR's past, Gordon is its future.

Stock car racing has spawned several national magazines and just as many weekly newspapers devoted to covering the goings on within the Winston Cup circuit and all affiliated series. Moreover, two community colleges in North Carolina are soon to offer two-year degree programs in motorsports management and marketing.

NASCAR's growth hasn't been without some problems, though. In 1996, the series held its last race at the North Wilkesboro Speedway, a half-mile track that was one of the charter members of the NASCAR organization. Its limited seating and close proximity to larger tracks in Charlotte, Martinsville and

Darlington made it a victim of growth. The owners of New Hampshire International Speedway and the Texas Motor Speedway bought the track for its two annual dates. Those events have been shifted to the larger facilities. Each year new tracks are built, though NASCAR maintains an expansion of the season is not in the works. Some of the older facilities may again fall at the expense of some of the racing palaces being built around the country.

Fan interaction with the drivers — a key to the sport's fan-friendly approach — has been limited in recent years due to the increased demand on the drivers. France has stressed that this interaction is an important aspect to racing and vows to continue the open-garage approach. No other sport allows fans to enter the locker rooms before a big game. NASCAR, to some extent, allows that to occur each and every week.

How big the sport can get before hitting its pinnacle remains the big question.

Television ratings for the sport continue to increase on an annual basis and most tracks can't build enough seats to accommodate the fan demand. And sponsor interest also doesn't seem to be waning, yet.

But there are some, albeit minor, signs of maturation of the business.

In the beginning, there were many independent teams who took part in the first stages of growth in the sport. But, as financial demands and the level of competition has increased, there has been some consolidation. Some smaller teams have merged or sold out to larger ones and others have simply closed up and gone out of business.

Same holds true for the collectible side of the business. Once the domain of mom and pop retailers, collectibles marketing is going big time. There's already been a consolidation of some collectibles manufacturers. And the effect of NASCAR's own licensed stores on those smaller retailers remains to be seen. However, because more products are available, selling an item isn't as easy as it was five years ago.

Much the way it has occurred in traditional businesses, vertical integration has become a buzzword in the racing world. In the past teams would contract out for engines, public relations help, show car programs and other functions; now many are supplying those operations in house. That change, of course, makes it harder for companies doing those jobs on an outside basis to survive.

Without further expansion of the schedule into new regions of the country, NASCAR will have to build upon the blocks it already has. Some of those plans are in place already. Executives are now expanding the brand to raise revenue by lending the NASCAR name to new products or ventures.

The NASCAR Craftsman Truck Series, started in 1995, is one such example of extending the core brand into a new area, without taxing the main business of Winston Cup racing. More recently, NASCAR has cut deals with autoparts companies to lend its name to a line of products sold to consumers. There again, the company is expanding its name recognition, raising cash, and not lowering the value of the top level of the sport. The NASCAR Cafes and NASCAR Thunder stores fall into the same category.

These signals of maturation notwithstanding, there's every indication that the peak is still a long way off. The addition of new tracks in Texas and California will certainly enlarge NASCAR's fan base. And with the marketing of a new crop of young drivers, like Gordon, as rivals to young stars in other sports, new fans will soon enter the fray.

Though NASCAR has grown dramatically in the half century it has been in existence, many of the basic tenets set by William Henry Getty France in 1947 remain the same: Good close racing, parity among teams, fan-friendly drivers and new-looking cars. For that, France, Sr. may have been the most important man in the history of American motorsports.

By all accounts, NASCAR racing has yet to reach its peak. Figuring out when it will is best left to economics gurus. Using television ratings as a yardstick, some 8.3 million television homes tuned into the 1997 Daytona 500, the sport's biggest event. The 1997 Super Bowl was watched in 42 million homes. Can NASCAR ever expect Super Bowl-like ratings for the annual telecast of the Daytona 500 or any other race?

Only time will answer that question. However, one thing is certain: NASCAR racing is the sport of the '90s.

Fact is, it's the fastest-growing sport in America. Hold on and enjoy the ride.

THE CARS

NASCAR's Steel Chariots

Looks can be deceiving.

A Winston Cup stock car looks a lot like the family sedan, yet it's anything but. "There's nothing stock about a stock car," so the frequently repeated phrase goes. There are few truer statements in racing.

Today's high speed racers bear few similarities to their showroom brethren. Aside from the body shape and size, there isn't much interchangeable between a 1996 Chevrolet Monte Carlo found at a local car dealer and the one driven by Dale Earnhardt on the NASCAR circuit.

Fact is, racing has come a long way from its early days when the cars — with minor safety alterations — raced exactly the way they came off of the showroom floor.

"When I started racing they were absolutely stock," said Ned Jarrett, a two-time NASCAR points champion who started in 1953. "I drove the car to the race track never considering I might have to tow it home if the engine blew up."

The stock aspect dates back to the early days of organized racing, which was in the late '40s. The sport's roots are firmly entrenched in the back roads of the South when moonshine runners raced against each other in fields when they weren't trying to outrun law enforcement officials. Those early races were run in fields and without any of the accoutrements available to drivers or fans today. The basic goals, however, were the same: to prove who was fastest.

Stock car racing got its formal start in 1947, when Bill France, Sr., a mechanic from Washington, D.C., convinced some friends to back his effort to organize the sport of racing. A December 12, 1947, meeting resulted in the creation of the National Association for Stock Car Automobile Racing. The first NASCAR-sanctioned race ever was held in Daytona Beach on February 15, 1948. As the name states, the cars were similar to those purchased by average folks.

In the early days, the cars remained stock, with the few changes permitted. A roll cage, made with plumber's tubing, was one of the few safety features incorporated into the race cars of the '50s. The bars were rudimentary at best and a far cry from the extensive safety cages built into today's cars. Seat belts weren't required in cars until 1953 and were limited to the simple lap belt offered in street vehicles. Drivers wore short-sleeved shirts — just as they did on the streets — and crude helmets. Some drivers actually drove cars with back seats and carpeted floors. Safety was clearly an afterthought.

NASCAR racing slowly started moving away from the strictly stock cars in the early '60s. Even then, with cars moving at speeds of over 150 mph, some drivers had vehicles with functioning doors and minimal internal roll bars.

Car technology underwent its greatest changes in the '70s, during a period in which the auto manufacturers were supporting factory-owned teams. The automakers lived by the axiom, "Win on Sunday, sell on Monday." In theory, fans bought the cars that were fastest during the races on Sunday. As a result, the manufacturers, hoping to lure buyers, did everything they could to make sure their cars were out in front when the checkered flag fell on Sunday afternoon.

NASCAR exploited America's love affair with automobiles and the manufacturers piled on. Indeed, one of the basic tenets of stock car racing is that the cars competing on the track — or a reasonable replica — be available to fans through their local auto dealers. Under NASCAR's early rules, a minimum of 500 of each model was to be made available for sale to the general public. Through the mid-'70s, the nation's automakers took that part of NASCAR's rules verbatim and created a few cars that were designed just for racing. Showroom sales were something that was necessary to get the car into competition, although Detroit produced just enough to meet NASCAR's minimum requirements. The 1969 Dodge Charger and Plymouth SuperBird are examples of what occurred when a manufacturer tried to build cars for racing only.

"The manufacturers were making special cars," said Jarrett. "They had to make 500, but that wasn't enough for each dealer to get one car. They were getting pretty exotic. NASCAR saw the direction it was headed and put a stop to it."

The sanctioning body eventually changed the rule to state that manufacturers had to build at least 1,000 cars or a number equal to one-half the number of dealerships of any given model in order for the car to race. More recently, in 1986, Chevrolet introduced a slope-backed Monte Carlo SS specifically for racing. A limited edition was offered for sale to the public, effectively skirting NASCAR's rule. Today, NASCAR's rules call for production volume models.

NASCAR has prided itself on keeping the competition on an equal level for all participants. One way it ensured parity was by forcing the manufacturers to stick with showroom models. If they hadn't, the manufacturers would have continued to create elaborate racing machines in an attempt to get a leg up on the competition.

The level of competition has also been kept on the same plane by limiting technological advances that have permeated — and some say damaged — other forms of motorsports. Indy car and Formula One racing rely heavily on computer-controlled devices. Such technology gives the drivers more information while in the car and helps them perform several functions during the race. It also allows crews to know exactly how the car is handling, enabling them to plan specific changes during pit stops. Open-wheel Indy cars, such as those run by Championship Auto Racing Teams and the new Indy Racing League, incorporate data acquisition computers which relay such information as suspension travel, oil pressure, speed, and fuel pressure. Information generated by the computer sensors spaced at locations around the car is transferred to the driver and to the crew members in the pits.

By limiting such technology in stock car racing, NASCAR has so far avoided a situation that exists in open-wheel racing, where there are clearly "haves" and "have nots" — the former, of course, being those teams whose owners have an abundance of money which can be sunk into research and development. Developing and advancing computer technology on race cars is a costly proposition.

"Everybody has a better wheel, so to speak," said Kevin Triplett, Winston Cup manager of communications. "Before you know it you're spending as much on [computers] as you are on the cars. We don't want it to be black-box technology. We want the black box to be in the driver's head and in his right foot. When the final data is processed, we want the driver to be making the decision."

To date, NASCAR has been successful in keeping its competitors on the same level. Sure, there are some teams that are better funded than others — the multi-car teams of Rick Hendrick, Jack Roush and Robert Yates are the leaders that come to mind. However, because of the sanctioning body's technological limitations, even those teams with more money are unable to introduce computer technology that would blow away the less-funded teams in the field.

It's no secret that underneath the various manufacturers' sheet metal bodies, the cars are virtually the same. The main difference, of course, is the motor, and even there, because of NASCAR's rules, the differences can be very small.

Under NASCAR's current rules all Winston Cup cars must have an overall wheel-base of 110 inches. Maximum height is 51 inches. The engines are 358 c.i. V-8, which are fitted with Holley 750-830 CFM 4-barrel carburetors. They run on 108 octane gasoline provided free of charge at the track by Unocal. Each car is equipped with a 22-gallon flexible fuel cell which is enclosed within a sheet metal frame secured within the chassis in the rear of the vehicle. The cars use four-wheel disc brakes and 9.5x15 wheels.

"Some of the things haven't changed," said Jarrett. "The basic chassis being used today is the same basic chassis that was being used 30 years ago. NASCAR found a concept that worked and they stayed with it. I admire them for that."

The groundwork for each model is the same: a rectangular steel tube chassis which includes a multi-point roll cage designed to protect the drivers in case of an accident. The roll cage in today's racers is made of 1 3/4" steel tubing, which is designed in parts to absorb the energy of a crash, while other parts are ridged to protect the driver.

The cars use independent coil spring twin control arms in the front steering mechanism. The rear suspension is called a "full floating axle," which consists of trailing arms — steel bars connected to the chassis and the axle — coil springs and a panhard rod.

Whereas the early race cars were direct decedents of their showroom siblings, today's cars at best could be considered very distant cousins.

NASCAR has approved six body types for competition — the Chevrolet Monte Carlo, the Oldsmobile Cutlass Supreme, the Buick Regal, the Ford Thunderbird, the Pontiac Grand Prix, and the Mercury Cougar. A vast majority of the teams use the Monte Carlo, with the bulk of the rest using Thunderbirds. A few teams use the Grand Prix.

The street versions of these cars are very similar to each other in terms of general operation, motor size and features.

However, in head-to-head comparisons with race cars, the differences between showroom stock and NASCAR vehicles is dramatic. Here's a sampling of the differences. The Monte Carlo and Grand Prix are both front-wheel drive, while the racing versions maintain the rear-wheel drive chassis of their roots. The street versions are a few inches taller than their racing cousins. The street versions incorporate 231 c.i. six-cylinder engines producing 240 hp, while the race cars use eight-cylinder 358 c.i. powerplants producing up to 750 hp. Street cars use five quarts of motor oil; race cars use 15. And the street cars incorporate electronic fuel injection, while the race cars use normally aspirated engines with carburetors.

A typical Winston Cup team will have at least 10 cars ready to go at any given time. In general, there's a primary and backup car available for the four types of tracks on the NASCAR circuit: Superspeedways (Talladega, Daytona), intermediates (Charlotte, Atlanta), short tracks (Bristol, Martinsville) and road courses (Sears Point, Watkins Glen).

Teams build the cars to meet the specific characteristics of each type of track. Superspeedway cars are built to be aerodynamically efficient. Short track cars are designed with the maximum amount of weight to the driver's side for easier turning. Road course cars balance the weight throughout the car to accommodate both right and left turns. And intermediate cars are built to create the greatest amount of down force, while still being aerodynamically efficient.

Anti-stock car fans are quick to point out the differences between the street versions and their high-speed relatives as a way to argue labeling the sport "stock" a mistake. However, NASCAR's conscious decision not to keep up with today's technology is one made to keep advancement of racing within the hands of the men working on the cars day in and day out.

Observers of the sport maintain that if the technological doors were opened, the future of the sport would fall into the hands of those car owners who could afford to operate vast computer laboratories to generate radically new advances. Those changes could, no doubt, dramatically alter the shape of stock car racing.

Anyone doubting NASCAR's concern with a level playing field need look no further than the ongoing Ford and Chevrolet aerodynamic battle of the past few seasons. In 1995, after years of the Ford Thunderbird having a perceived aerodynamic advantage over the Chevrolet Lumina, Chevy introduced the Monte Carlo. Almost overnight, the aerodynamic advantage shifted from the Fords to the Chevys. Ford brass and teams balked, forcing NASCAR to address the situation. Over time, NASCAR continually made minor adjustments to both the Ford and Chevy body styles, as well as their spoiler and airdam heights. By the end of the 1996 season it appeared the gap between the two makes had closed. Still, well into the 1997 season, NASCAR continued to equalize the Chevy and Ford teams.

Likewise, NASCAR has allowed Pontiac teams to use a non-stock snout to try to eliminate aerodynamic differences between the Pontiacs and the other makes.

Still, such dedication to a level playing field has left teams little room to gain an advantage over the next guy. In the '70s and '80s, when the Detroit muscle cars were the rage, teams would build bigger motors. But, with speeds soaring and the risk of a car sailing into the stands in a major wreck, NASCAR moved to limit the motors to the current 358 c.i. version.

"NASCAR's rules are so stringent that any of the technology that is out there today is stuff we're not allowed to use," said Rusty Wallace, driver of the Penske South-owned Miller Brewing Ford Thunderbird. "As far as calculating fuel mileage, when a driver runs himself right to the end and runs out of fuel, they don't know how long it's going to run. We could put fuel meters in there with no problem and we could tell exactly how much fuel is left in the car, but that's not allowed.

"We could have all kinds of things that are not allowed. The technology available right now through Penske North (the Indy car operation of Penske racing) and the engineering team on the IndyCar team is unbelievable, but you can't use any of it in Winston Cup. We're being restrained. But if it controls the cost of the cars and the action that NASCAR puts on, I think everybody would have to say it's a step above everything."

According to seven-time Winston Cup champion Dale Earnhardt, the money being spent on a Formula One team is about 20 times what's being spent on the average Winston Cup team, although the end result is the same — everyone wants to win.

Formula One, where the top teams operate on a budget of about $50 million, is heavily dependent on technology and computers. However, Earnhardt said that with the current growth of stock car racing he can see where the sport could fall into the same big-buck trap.

"But the reason it doesn't go like Formula One or IndyCar racing is that NASCAR puts limitations on what you can do," Earnhardt said. "They need to keep doing that to keep the price tag down and to keep technology to a workable level to where guys can do it and it doesn't take as many high-dollar guys to be able to do it."

Robert Yates, who fields cars driven by Ernie Irvin and Dale Jarrett, agrees that it's getting tougher to find speed within the confines of NASCAR's guidelines, although he believes there are ways to make the cars go faster.

"We've got to keep figuring out how to keep optimizing these little areas," Yates said. "It won't come in big packages — a little horsepower here, a little bit of drag there . . . There's still a lot of freedom. All of a sudden something clicks in the middle of the night; the fear is that if you go to sleep you'll forget it."

Car Building

Building a car takes about 80 man days, according to Clyde Booth, operations manager for Mark Rypien Motorsports, which fields John Deere-backed Pontiacs for Chad Little.

It can be can be done faster, if say, the driver wrecked the best car last weekend and the team needs to use it next weekend. Under those conditions, a race car can be built rapidly to meet a deadline. But in a non-rushed situation, it'll take nearly two weeks to construct a car from the ground up.

The cornerstone of any stock car is the chassis. Most of the larger teams — Wallace, Hendrick, Roush Racing, etc. — build their own chassis in house. Others, such as Rypien Motorsports buy theirs from an outside manufacturer such as Ronnie Hopkins Enterprises, Laughlin Race Products or Hutcherson-Pagen Enterprises.

A chassis is constructed from 600 lbs of tubular steel and sheet metal, according to Ronnie Hopkins, Jr., president of RHE. Tubing to form the roll cage is cut from 20-foot lengths, bent and then welded into places specified by the team. The overall construction of the chassis is generally the same, although teams can select the type of front suspension unit they want — usually referred to as the front clip — and the rear portion, known as the rear clip.

It takes between 45 and 70 man hours to build each chassis, Hopkins said. They're delivered to the teams with a frame, roll cage and interior sheet metal, such as the floorpan, which is designated by NASCAR.

Once the chassis arrives at Rypien's shop, two men will spend four days installing such parts as brake brackets, throttle brackets, steering mounts, fuel cell mounts and shock mounts, Booth said. They'll also take the time to verify the front-end geometry to make sure all parts of the chassis are lined up. If they go forward without making such a check and the chassis is out of line, it will be difficult to find the problem later on.

"A critical dimension could be 300,000ths of an inch," Booth said. "Some vary 200,000ths. We have to physically go and check them."

Once those parts are completed and checked, the car is moved to a different area of the shop where two men will spend seven to 10 days creating the body. The roof, the hood and the rear decklid are the only body parts on the car that are stock. The remainder of the body is hand crafted out of sheet metal, with the front fascia and the rear bumper being made of composite materials.

"A speedway car will take about 10 days," Booth said. "It's a lot more critical."

Any divots in the body or parts that do not fit snugly on a speedway car will create wind resistance when it is on the track and ultimately scrub off speed in a sport where the starting positions can be decided by thousandths of a second.

When the body is complete, the car is moved to another portion of the shop, where much of the interior work is done. Four men will spend five days installing the seat, dashboard, firewall and wiring systems. At the same time, the interior aluminum parts are being created and installed. These parts include rear and front crush panels, which are parts designed to keep exhaust fumes out of the driver's compartment, the shroud covering the radiator and spoilers. The front and rear windows are made by an outside company, though are trimmed to fit. Side and rear panel windows are custom made in house.

After all of the parts have been made and installed, the car is totally stripped down, leaving just the body and the chassis. The car is moved to the body shop where two men will spend three days applying paint. The inside of the car is painted first and then the outside, said Booth.

With the cosmetics part of the process complete, the car is then ready for final assembly. Four men will spend five days putting the car back together. The custom made aluminum parts, the cooling system, the rear end, the brake system, the engine, transmission, and the steering mechanism will all be installed.

"The car is then ready for set up," Booth said. "This will usually take two men about a day. We'll weigh it to make sure we've got the wheel weights where we want them."

During this process, the team will add 250-350 lbs of lead to bring the car up to NASCAR's approved weight limits. (For the 1997 season, NASCAR is factoring the weight of the driver into the overall weight of the car. In the past, cars needed to weight 3,400 lbs, with no more than 1,600 lbs being located on the driver's side of the car. Now NASCAR is requiring drivers weighing less than 200 lbs to add an amount of lead to the car to make them equal to that figure. Drivers weighting 200 lbs won't have to add weight. However, a driver weighing 150 lbs will have to add 50 lbs to the overall weight of the car, bringing the total up to 3,450 lbs.)

At the same time the crew is fixing the weight of the car, they'll also set the front end height, set the weight balance of the car, and make final adjustments based on levels learned through testing. After the final set-up stage, one man will spend about half a day cleaning and waxing the car.

The car will cost about $75,000, without an engine. An engine costs roughly $40,000. According to Booth, the cost of the car without an engine breaks down to about $40,000 in parts and $35,000 in labor.

Engines

The basic cast-iron block engine in stock cars today is very similar to the same one first introduced to racing in 1958. That's about where the similarities end. Today's powerplants are high-speed beasts capable of churning out 750 hp.

The engine is the heart of a Winston Cup car. As such, it's where many teams spend a sizeable portion of their overall budgets.

The larger teams on the Winston Cup circuit build their own engines. Doing so gives them the flexibility to try new parts and to consistently experiment. Others simply buy or lease their motors.

Winston Cup engine builders rarely divulge their actual horsepower outputs, though engine builders say GM motors generate about 740 hp, while Ford motors hit 750 hp. About 85 percent of the total horsepower output of an engine makes it to the rear wheels.

At any given time, Bahari Racing will have 20 motors on hand, according to chief engine builder, Ron Puryear. Of those engines, six will be built for restrictor plate races, three are engines with 9:1 compression ratios for Busch cars, and a dozen will be built for all other Winston Cup events.

About 160 man hours go into building a racing engine. The block and the heads are purchased from General Motors or Ford. Teams order the blocks and heads from the manufacturer, which are machined to each team's specifications. All other parts purchased from outside suppliers, such as the fuel pump, are taken apart and prepped before being installed on the motor.

Once the motor is built, it's mounted on on a dynamometer, which measures horsepower, often called brake horsepower.

To generate more horsepower, engine builders look for ways to reduce frictional losses inside the engine, such as those that exist between the cylinder walls and the piston rings. From there, they'll work on the manifolds and valves.

"The biggest advances have been in the scientific research in heads and manifolds," Puryear said. "You work to have an increased amount of air and fuel input, which leads to more horsepower."

Of all the areas of a Winston Cup shop, the engine room was one of the first to step into the computer age. Aside from the dynometers used to test horsepower, teams use computer-controlled equipment to assure that they can repeatedly duplicate key engine parts. Despite that equipment, there is still room for advancement and tinkering, according to Yates, who is considered one of the premiere engine builders in the business.

Indeed, even with the new technology, it is difficult for engine builders to create two engines alike. Yates often builds 20 engines before getting the two that will power the cars of Ernie Irvan and Dale Jarrett each week. And finding what causes the differences between equally prepared motors is just as difficult as building the motors in the first place, he said.

"We have digital equipment that measures down to the millionths of inches," he said, "Still, we're dealing with air and a lot of different pressures. If we build 20 engines the same way, there will be a 15 horsepower spread among them."

On the track, every extra 7 hp a builder can squeeze out of an engine should result in the car going one mph hour faster.

"You keep working on them," Yates said. "There's a lot going on in an engine. We're constantly studying them."

"You're dealing with the thermal characteristics of the block," said Puryear. "The rigidity of one block can be slightly different from the other. Frictional losses can vary from one engine to the next."

The area that gives engine builders their biggest headaches and can drive a builder batty is working with restrictor plate motors.

NASCAR introduced the plates — which sit between the intake manifold and the carburetor — in 1988 as a way to cut speeds on superspeedways. When it became the norm for cars to average laps of 200 mph at tracks like Talladega and Daytona, NASCAR moved to slow the cars down. The faster speeds created the potential for more serious injuries during what has become routine multi-car melees. In addition, the speeds increased the risk of a car going airborne and potentially landing in the grandstands. NASCAR had such a scare in 1987 when Bobby Allison's car sailed into a catch fence at Talladega and nearly went into the stands.

Restrictor plates cut about 300 hp from the motor, resulting in speeds about 189 mph at Daytona and Talladega.

While cutting horsepower, the plates also result in more work for Winston Cup engine builders. Teams will spend more than half of their annual engine budget trying to offset the horsepower loss effect of the restrictor plates.

"Restrictor plate racing requires an extra month or so just to get the engines ready," said team owner and three time Winston Cup champion Darrell Waltrip.

"As soon as the season ends," Puryear said, "the entire month of December and January are totally consumed trying to develop two or three more horsepower."

In an effort to help reduce the amount of money teams spend on engines, in 1996 NASCAR required teams to run motors with a 14:1 compression ratio for races at Daytona and Talladega. In 1997, that rule was extended to all engines for all tracks. Before, teams would run engines with compression ratios as high as 18:1, which, while producing more power, also caused more engine failures.

So far, engine builders haven't noticed a significant loss in horsepower. It's simply another rule they've got to abide by.

"You are certainly restricted and sometimes hampered," Puryear said of NASCAR's rules. "Associated with racing is the common term, speed. Also associated with racing is creativity, and sometimes rules limit one's creativeness."

Aerodynamics-Testing-Racing

Not since the early '70s, when Dodge and Plymouth decided to make aerodynamics a factor with the introduction of the winged Chargers and SuperBirds, has the topic been as relevant as it has been in the '90s.

As NASCAR has worked to limit horsepower and keep car bodies as close to stock dimensions as possible, car manufacturers and teams have sought to make their cars sleeker and more wind resistant on the track. Teams now spend thousands of dollars each year refining the way their cars slip through the air.

No matter how large the engine in the car, how it cuts through the air is an extremely important factor in racing. In the late '60s and early '70s, racers focused most of their energy on building bigger, stronger engines. But towards the end of the '60s, the auto manufacturers started examining the effects of aerodynamics on stock cars. Chrysler, which had seen its cars beaten week in and week out by the sloped-back Fords and Mercurys, came up with the idea of creating a car with a smooth front and a large wing on the back. Chrysler's winged Dodge Charger appeared in competition for the first time midway through the 1969 season at Talladega.

Despite the Chrysler experiments, it wasn't until the '80s when aerodynamics became a serious factor in race car, or street car, design.

Racing's aerodynamic efforts are, in part, aided by the auto manufacturers in Detroit who for years have tried to make passenger cars more efficient on the highways. One way of reducing gas consumption, of course, is lowering the amount of force it takes for a car to move through the air.

Aerodynamics became a hot-button topic in 1995 when Chevrolet introduced the Monte Carlo, which by all accounts was a much more aerodynamically superior car to its predecessor the Lumina. The Monte Carlo had less wind resistance — or drag as it's referred to by engineers — than did the Ford Thunderbird, which had been the proven leader in the category. The design of the Monte Carlo, as approved by NASCAR, also provided teams with more rear-end down force, which allowed a Chevy driver to stay on the gas longer going through the turns.

Throughout the 1995, 1996, and 1997 seasons, NASCAR instituted various rules for all models — usually dealing with the height of front and rear spoilers — that were designed to make all of the cars as equal as possible.

The general consensus among drivers and crew chiefs is that the Chevy and Ford teams are now closer in performance, while the Pontiac is in need of additional refinements.

When dealing with aerodynamics, teams strive for the perfect combination of low air resistance and ultimate down force, which will allow the car to move freely through the air while maintaining a grip on the track surface.

A team's first step at aerodynamic efficiency occurs in the body shop where every ding, divot and crease is filled in and smoothed over. The next part of the process is a trip to a wind tunnel either in Detroit or one of those at the major aeronautics operations in the south.

In the wind tunnel, cars are placed on four pads connected to a computer system. The car is then subject to wind speeds up to 200 mph, which will simulate race action and allow crews to detect how the car may react on the track. Engineers also use fan-blown smoke to see how wind flows over, under and around a stock car. Using the various tests, crews can find the body style and shape that is most effective.

During the typical test, teams will spend eight hours in a wind tunnel at a cost of roughly $20,000.

"Before we go to the wind tunnel we sit down and decide what we want to work on," Deere's Booth said. "From there we develop a game plan."

Prior to a session in wind tunnel, most teams usually build several configurations of each of the body parts they've set out to test. This may include fenders, snouts, quarter panels or rear decks.

NASCAR's current template system leaves some, albeit little, room for body shape manipulation, although some areas still remain for teams to tinker.

"On a speedway car, testing is just a game of a 16th of an inch here and a 100th of an inch there to gain a second," Booth said.

"Your overall body shape is very consistent," said Jeff Hammond, crew chief for Western Auto-backed Darrell Waltrip Motorsports. "But you still have areas where you need to pay attention. It will drive a man crazy at night, during the day, whatever, thinking about ways to reshape a panel, to reshape a car — and still meet the required template."

Once in the wind tunnel, engineers look for ways to reduce drag. Drag, the amount of force compared to the size of the object, is measured in counts. In the wind tunnel, seven counts is equal to one mph on the track.

They'll attempt to lower those counts with the reconfigured body parts. Occasionally, according to Booth, teams will also try their body styles with the snouts or other parts from different brands in order to test what their competitors have.

"Everything now is taken to the Nth degree," Hammond said. "It's as if we're in the military and we're building a stealth bomber. Can we shave this? Can we make it sharper?"

Trying to shave off speed aerodynamically is getting tougher, however, according to Doug Hewitt, crew chief for Pennzoil-backed Bahari Racing.

Indeed, for the 1997 season, NASCAR required that teams mount the rear quarter panels up one inch higher than they did in 1996, which has resulted in cars having 10 more counts of drag, Hewitt said.

"You're always working to get more horsepower," Hewitt said. "And you're always working to get them as smooth as you can. When you work in the wind tunnel, you try and get the car as best you can. It's a baseline. You can tell [in the wind tunnel] if you're in the ballpark or not. By going to the wind tunnel we can get a good idea of what to expect out of the car."

What the wind tunnel can't do, however, is factor in the effects of a car actually moving on the track. In race conditions, the tires move in and out of the fender wells, resulting in more drag and lost speed. Under normal conditions, chassis flex also alters the aerodynamic properties of a car.

Those questions that can't be answered in the wind tunnel are usually answered at the track in various test sessions teams will stage throughout the season and during pre-race practice periods. NASCAR allows teams seven three-day tests at tracks that host Winston Cup events. Most teams will use two of their annual allotment in preparation for the Daytona 500 in February. Some will take part in tire tests for Goodyear, although those sessions usually generate little in the way of information for the teams.

"What you do, whether it's Talladega or Daytona," Hewitt said, "is work on aerodynamics and qualifying set up. You will play with all aspects of the car, aerodynamics, springs, shocks and engines. You try to find the best combination that is the fastest."

Testing also gives teams a chance to work with any new rules NASCAR may have instituted during the off season. For example, before the 1997 season started, the sanctioning body added a new rule designed to limit the use of soft springs at the superspeedways. While the soft springs made it possible for cars to meet NASCAR's height requirements, during the race the air pressure on the car would lower the overall level of the vehicle and cut down on drag.

But at the start of 1997, before measuring a car's height, NASCAR added a 75 lb weight to both sides of the rear of the car. However, by the time the series rolled into Talladega in April, the 75-lb rule had been eliminated.

"It's basically pretty simple," Hammond said of testing. "No. 1 is to make the car as fast as possible. If you can achieve the first, you want to work on race configurations."

To help speed up the testing process, teams incorporate fairly sophisticated on-board data acquisition computers. The systems are prohibited in competition, although NASCAR allows teams to use them in testing situations.

Before practicing, sensors are placed around the car to measure such details as ride height, engine exhaust and intake levels, air pressure levels at the front and rear of the car, rpm, mph, and the angles of the wheels. The information from the sensors is downloaded into a computer which then simulates the car's movement around the track.

"If you have a problem you can identify the problem faster," Booth said. "Without the computers a lot of times you have to guess."

In the absence of on-board computers, teams are forced to rely on the driver's explanation of the way the car is handling. For some drivers, translating what they're feeling in the seat of the car to their crew chiefs is a difficult task.

"When I was with Darrell Waltrip," Booth said, "he would come in and say the problem is in the left front. A lot of drivers can't do that."

"You can look at testing to learn different things," Chad Little said. "It all depends on what track it is. Sometimes you might test for driver experience. But 90 percent of the time you go out with a hit list of a page, page and a half, of the things you might want to try because we hear other teams are trying it; or it might be other ideas the guys want to try, or it might be a trend. Most of the time you try to get the car as close as possible so that 99 percent of the time when we unload it off the truck [before a race] it's as fast as it can be."

Testing usually involves drivers taking countless laps around the track, sometimes alone, sometimes in packs. Each time out the team is trying something slightly different from the last. For instance, running in packs will let the driver know how the car is going to handle in traffic. Alone will give the driver an idea of how the car may qualify.

On the larger tracks, specifically the superspeedways, cars are affected by what's called the draft. In general, two cars running nose-to-tail can run much faster than one alone. When one car is moving alone, it breaks through the air which then flows over the top of the car and down on the rear spoiler. That downward pressure at the rear of the car, combined with a swirling effect of the air directly behind the car, will pull back slightly on the car.

A second car running behind the first is pulled into a vacuum of sorts in the air coming off the first car. This allows the second car to go just as fast without exerting as much force as the first. The result is a pushing effect on the first car, which makes the two move swiftly together. Before restrictor plates were introduced, the second car in a draft would have a significant advantage over the first because he wasn't using all of the power he had. As such, drivers would gain momentum in the draft and then pull down on the track and pass the first car in a so-called slingshot move.

In testing and practice, drivers will attempt to draft with other makes of cars to find out where their car works best.

And once the series of laps are complete, the driver returns to the pits or garage area to go over the results with the crew.

"It's really redundant, most of the time," Little said.

Testing and practice sessions involve endless fiddling with the chassis, which, aside from the roll cage, is a somewhat complex marriage of metal. It's a system that could drive a physics professor crazy trying to perfect. However, as most race car drivers will say, there's no such thing as a perfect car. A set-up that feels comfortable in one turn, may not be right for the next. A car that's fast in the straights may handle terribly in the turns.

Getting a car comfortable for a driver all the way around the track is left up to a chassis specialist who, by manipulating such parts as shocks, springs, sway bars and steering components, can get the car suitable to the driver's needs.

During practice drivers will determine whether a car is neutral, if it's loose, or if it's pushing. In a loose car, the driver senses the rear of the car is breaking away from the pavement. A car with a push gives the driver the sensation of not being able to turn the car in corners. Ideally, a driver wants a neutral car, which will have neither a push nor feel loose.

Often a crew's first attempt at righting a car is with wedge, an adjustment of weight in the opposite corners of the vehicle. By slipping a ratchet though a hole in the rear window — there is one on each side of the car — a crew member can increase or decrease the amount of weight on a wheel under the ratchet. Adding more weight to the left rear wheel — the most common change made for a loose car — automatically impacts the weight to the right front wheel. The same holds true if weight is adjusted on the right rear wheel.

In practice, teams will often change shocks or springs in their search of the perfect set up. In recent years, shocks have become one of the most important parts of a car's chassis adjustments. Just as they do in street cars, the shocks in stock cars perform several functions. The most important is keeping the wheel in contact with the road surface. They also help keep the car from rolling sideways in the turns. Today, most team haulers are fitted with shock dynos making it possible for crew members to create shock combinations for specific tracks and race conditions while they are at the track.

Shocks ultimately work to control the compression and extension of the four coil springs, one on each corner of the car, which support the overall weight of the vehicle. Springs come in a variety of sizes and strengths. The softer a spring, the less support it will provide the car under stress. For example, in recent years, teams used soft rear springs on the superspeedways. Once up to race speeds, the force of the air rushing by would press down on the rear of the car, therefore cutting the wind away from the rear spoiler and cut drag.

Springs are measured in the amount of pounds of force per inch of deflection. Teams usually refer to them by the number of pounds, such as an 1,800-pound spring.

It's extremely rare that a spring would be changed during race action. However, teams often use small pieces of rubber — called donuts — to make adjustments to the springs during pit-stops. Once the car is jacked up and the tire removed, a crew member reaches in and slips the rubber between two coils on the spring. The effect should be a stiffening of the spring's reaction.

Also affecting the way a car handles is the camber and caster of the front wheels, which is the overall angle of the wheel. The goal is to get the largest portion of the tires in contact with the race track. One way of achieving this is by adjusting the right front wheel out slightly at the bottom, so that when the car enters the banking of the turns, the entire rubber surface is on the track. Caster and camber are adjusted using small metal shims that are installed on the A-arms, which are triangular pieces of metal that hold the ball joints in place with the wheel. There are two A-arms in place for each front wheel. Together they hold the balljoints and wheel spindles. A tire mounted on a hub is attached to the spindle.

In the rear end of the car, teams can adjust springs and shocks, as well as the track bar, or panhard bar, which controls the roll point of the rear end.

"Testing is a good time to try anything that you feel might benefit your team," Hammond said. "But it's a cloak and dagger type of deal. You are in an environment with some competitors and sharp people. You may not want to tip your hand on those things."

Every change a crew member makes to any one of the adjustable parts on the car will result in something else on the car handling differently. Indeed, the best chassis specialists will look at the overall picture — and what any change will make on the rest of the car — before making a minor adjustment.

"We're into geometry now," Hammond said. "We pay attention to detail. What happens when a car goes from a stationary ride height to a full ride height? We now understand what happens when the car flexes. It's the detail that has changed more than anything in racing. Ten, 15, 20 years ago we didn't worry about that. It used to be we'd bolt it together and go racing."

"Like everything, even airplanes, it's the same as it was 10 years ago, but the cars are a little more refined, a little easier to maneuver," said Buddy Baker, a former full-time driver turned TNN broadcaster. Baker, who retired from racing in 1990, still occasionally drives test cars for Rusty Wallace. "Let's face it — with the wind tunnels and whatnot, they've just about taken the guesswork out of it. It's now down to what you [the driver] tell the crew. I can remember starting 500 miles 10 years ago and saying, 'man, this is awful.' Now they're very consistent. The tires are perfect. It's easier to drive now."

Tires

Of all the factors playing into the performance of a Winston Cup car, the tire is the only area that is equal among all teams participating in the sport.

One team may be able to develop a better motor or figure out the perfect set up for a particular track. But what they'll have in common with every other team in the field is the tires.

In some ways tires may also be one of the most important factors in how a car handles on the track. Tires are the driver's connection with the track. How they react to the surface and what the driver feels through the steering wheel and the seat of his pants, is relayed back to the team and used to make adjustments on the car's handling.

When NASCAR started, the rules called for stock tires, and that's what they used — grooved street tires. Over time, the rules were altered to say stock-sized tires, but with racing rubber. Tire makers designed tires with specific racing rubber compounds that were cut — with grooves — to the same dimensions as the typical street tire of the day. When the super-speedways opened, however, NASCAR officials realized they needed specific racing tires to handle the abrasive nature of the surface and the high speeds. Those needs resulted in the fore-runner of today's racing slicks.

Cars use slick tires in order to get the largest possible amount of rubber on the racing surface. The more rubber in contact with the roadway, the better and safer the race. Obviously, this conflicts with what most people believe when dealing with their personal automobiles. Slick or bald tires are bad in those situations. Street tires need grooves to push away water during rain storms or other inclement weather. Since NASCAR doesn't run in the rain, grooves are unnecessary in racing.

Still, the "contact patch," or amount of rubber from all four tires reaching the ground at any moment, is about one square foot, according to Goodyear research.

Today, each team will use the same make and composition of tires approved by NASCAR. The Goodyear Tire & Rubber Company is the sole supplier of the tires used by the Winston Cup series. Goodyear has been involved with NASCAR for more than 40 years and with a few exceptions has been unchallenged as the only supplier to the series. During the 1996 season, Goodyear sold roughly 90,000 tires to competitors participating on the Winston Cup, Busch Grand National and Craftsman Truck Series. Each tire costs just over $346 each.

In early 1997, Goodyear solidified its position as the sole supplier to NASCAR's top three divisions through an exclusive deal with the sanctioning body.

Goodyear designs specific tires for each race track, according to Stu Grant, general manager for racing, worldwide.

When creating a tire for a new facility such as the new California Speedway or the Texas Motor Speedway, Goodyear engineers collect data on the kind of cars that will be used, their engine size, the wheel base, aerodynamic loading, the surface of the facility, and any rules that are mandated by the sanctioning body.

"From an engineering standpoint," Grant said, "we need to know what the tire sees in each one of those situations. The tire requirements for service at Daytona are much different from Martinsville. "

Once the pertinent data has been collected, engineers feed the information into a computer, which also has a digitized model of the track and the car. Through the computer, engineers are able to determine what kind of rubber compound is necessary for a given track.

In deciding on a compound, Goodyear attempts to balance safety and making a tire last one pitstop in competition. "You don't want to pit for tires before you run out of gas," Grant said.

Goodyear currently makes about 20 different codes — or tires — for NASCAR Winston Cup competition. While each is different, there are some general rules. To accommodate higher levels of stress and heat, right side tires are made from stronger compounds. Right side tires are also slightly larger than left side tires — called stagger — to make it easier for cars to turn the corners. On superspeedways, for example, left side tires are 87.9 inches in circumference while right side tires are 88.5 inches around. Also, left side tires on superspeedways are good for about 300 miles, while right side tires are good for 150 miles. Road course tires carry the same circumference for both sides of the car.

Tires used at Daytona and Talladega — the fastest tracks on the circuit — will have the highest load ratings of any Winston Cup products, while those used at Martinsville, a slower half-mile, will not carry the same strength. According to Goodyear data, Winston Cup tires are subject to 2.0 Gs of force in the turns at the Indianapolis Motor Speedway, which is twice the force a skydiver feels in freefall.

Goodyear is required to make a minimum number of tires for each team for each track. The number of mandated tires varies track by track and is based on the average usage for each facility. The figure is more for Daytona, where teams will practice for a week before the race, and less at Martinsville, where tires last a little longer. For instance, in 1996, Goodyear brought 1,900 left and right tires to Martinsville, 1,600 to Talladega, 1,500 to Dover, 2,200 to Charlotte and 2,200 to Indianapolis.

The biggest change in Winston Cup tire technology was the 1989 introduction of the radial tire into competition. Until then, all teams used bias-ply tires. In broad terms, the difference lies in the construction of the two tires. Both are made using layers of materials, with bias-ply tires having those materials placed at an angle to the rolling direction of the tire. Radial tires have the materials running across the tread.

"It was a major advancement in two areas," Grant said, "puncture resistance, there are now many, many fewer punctures. And dimensional stability, which is a tremendous asset in terms of keeping tire handling constant."

Unlike radials, bias-ply tires often changed in size during the course of a race.

To say the radial tire has had an impact would be an understatement. Just ask Darrell Waltrip. "The radial tire changed our sport," Waltrip said. "The tire is so unpredictable. We always talked about the bias-plys. The thing about a radial, when you miss the set up, the car is violent. The radials also changed the whole way racing is. Look at the race tracks. You used to be able to run high and low." Instead, Waltrip said, there is just one area to run on the track.

Winston Cup cars use a tire set up that has an outer tire and an inner liner. The outside tire, of course, is what holds the road. The inner liner is a safety device, which in the case of a flat should allow the driver to return to the pits. The inner liner has a slightly higher air pressure level than the outer tire. Often, drivers will complain of tires "equalizing" during a race, which produces a vibrating effect. Equalizing occurs when the inner and outer tires have the same air pressure.

Goodyear engineers are constantly upgrading and tinkering with the compounds that they use in each tire. They'll test the designs on computers and through on-track tire tests with top-running teams.

During race weekends, Goodyear monitors the performance of its tires in practice and the race. Leading up to race day, Goodyear staffers are located at the entrance of pit road. After each practice run, competitors stop for the technicians, who then measure the temperatures across the surface of the tires. Those figures help Goodyear judge whether the tire is working, but they'll also help the team figure out whether their car is set up correctly. A right front tire running hotter than the right rear may suggest an understeer — or push — situation.

"The goal," said Grant, "is to provide a nice consistent product that the driver is comfortable with. It's a driver comfort issue. You want the driver to be happy when he races the car. You can't have a tire that's extremely hard and generates little grip. You need to have a tire that is tractive enough, or grippy enough, but not too soft."

The goals, however, do change when there is competition from another tire manufacturer as there was in 1995 when Hoosier began supplying tires to Winston Cup teams. The entrance of Hoosier launched a full-scale tire war in which both manufacturers attempted to create the fastest tires.

"At the moment there is no competition," Grant said. "But it does change the way we develop tires. With competition it is certainly more directed in decreasing lap times in order to compete."

Following the Rules

No matter what a team tries, ultimately, the car must pass muster with NASCAR officials, who nowadays are scrupulous in their inspection of all cars.

After years of being criticized of favoritism combined with talk of flagrant cheating by some competitors, NASCAR has worked hard in recent years to eliminate many of the gray areas in its rulebook that at times allowed teams to find loopholes that may or may not have enhanced their performance.

Prior to every race, each car is closely inspected for any potential rules violations or safety shortcomings.

"When I started out, our overall inspection process consisted of one guy with a tape measure, who measured a couple of different things," Hammond said. "They had an overall long template and two height gauges. There was no such thing as cross templates or door templates. There were a few measurements they wanted you to adhere to. It was so vague, guys would cut windshields, recut and rechrome bumpers."

But the days of dramatically altering the shape or style of a stock car are over. NASCAR officials now use 14 to 15 different templates to measure each car's body shape. There is some level of tolerance built into each template, ranging from 1/8th of an inch in some parts up to 1/2 of an inch in others.

Engines are examined by officials who randomly select a cylinder on the engines for a pump test, which will tell them the overall displacement of the motor. And each carburetor is removed just prior to heading out on the track to assure it meets the series' guidelines.

NASCAR also requires that the top-three finishers at each event tear down their engines for inspection following the race. Fuel samples from the top-10 qualifiers and the top-10 finishers are examined to assure teams are using officially sanctioned Unocal racing gasoline.

In addition to the engine and templates, NASCAR checks every car's fuel cell, roll-bar configuration and materials, weight, spoiler angles, window opening size, wheel camber and whether the roof-flaps, designed to stop a car going airborne during an accident, are working properly.

NASCAR's stringent rules have made it harder for the teams to get creative in their interpretations, although it hasn't stopped them from being aggressive. And cheating hasn't been eliminated.

In 1995, NASCAR clamped down on cheating by instituting large fines for teams caught with illegal or unapproved materials. Because inspectors are looking more closely to what teams are doing, the way they've tried to fool those inspectors has gotten downright ingenious.

During preparations for the 1995 Daytona 500, Bill Davis Racing was fined $25,000 for having a hydraulic device hooked up to lower the spoiler during the race.

Since then there have been other infractions ranging from having holes drilled into portions of the roll cage — done to lower overall weight — to having portions of the car fashioned out of solid steel to add weight to the car. In 1996, for example, one team was fined for having an ignition box made of steel in the driver's compartment.

"I'll tell you," Baker said. "With [series director] Gary Nelson and his crew down there, if you want to get ahead of him you've got to get up pretty early in the morning."

Being branded a cheater could do serious damage to a team today. Sponsors are paying millions of dollars to be associated with the sport. NASCAR makes public the names and fines levied against any team caught with illegal parts. As a result, a team's sponsor is mentioned along with the infraction.

"First off, these guys will do anything for 10 or 15 lbs of an advantage," Baker said, "which is, quite frankly, not going to win the race for you. They're almost cosmetic."

Still, within NASCAR's rules evolution, teams can find ways to make their cars faster without facing stiff and embarrassing fines. It's certainly not easy, though it can be done.

"You challenge whatever rules they come up with," Hammond said. "With the powers that be at NASCAR the gray area is shrinking fast. Each year they cut down what we can do. Because they restrict those areas, it opens new doors we might not have ever looked in. It's a continual chess game. Every time we make a move, they counter. Every time they make a move, we counter."

3

THE DRIVERS

A Thirst for Victory

Everyone thinks they can be a stock car driver.

That may be a gross exaggeration, but it's true that many race fans believe they could simply strap into a stock car — or even an Indy car — and drive off as the next Dale Earnhardt, Ricky Craven, Morgan Shepherd or Jeff Gordon.

This fantasy stems from Americans' love affair with their automobiles. Face it, just about everyone who owns a driver's license has mashed the gas in the family sedan on a deserted highway late at night. We've all done it. And who hasn't looked over at the driver in the next lane while waiting at a stoplight and thought, "I'll beat 'em off the line?"

But this is where auto racing is different from other sports. Few people sit around watching football and think they could actually be Dan Marino or Steve Young. With stick-and-ball sports — those covered heavily by the sports sections of most newspapers — there's a built-in belief that the participants have an athletic ability beyond the average person.

Yet anyone can drive a stock car. Yeah, right.

Being a race car driver takes a lot more than being able to go fast in a straight line on an empty highway. Becoming a Winston

Cup driver requires years of racing experience, an unquenchable desire to win, stamina and the ability to serve as a representative for a team and sponsor.

"You've got to be a winner," said Buddy Baker, a former driver turned TNN broadcaster. "Mental attitude has a great deal to do with a driver. If he questions his ability when he goes on a race track, he's not going to be very good. Race car drivers are borderline cocky. There's a little bit of arrogance that goes with it."

Three-time Winston Cup champion Darrell Waltrip, one of the sport's most enduring figures, has seen a few drivers come and go during his 25 years in the business. The good ones, he said, have a deep desire to excel.

"Every driver I've ever known, they're hungry," he said. "They want to be the next Darrell Waltrip. They've got that fire in their belly."

If there's a common thread running through today's Winston Cup drivers it's that a majority of them started young, very young. Either by desire or perhaps with a small push from their parents, they were around racing well before they could do long division. And for most, once they were in, they were in for life.

Gordon, the 1995 Winston Cup champion, may actually be one of the best and most successful examples of a driver starting out young. When he was 4 1/2 years old he was driving quarter-midget race cars. He continued racing and advancing upward — sometimes years ahead of other drivers his own age — to the point where he's considered one of the best drivers around. Several others started out the same way, progressing to stock cars as soon as they were old enough to drive street cars.

Those who didn't race as youngsters were usually around the sport in some way during their formative years. When they weren't in school, they could be found working on a race car alongside their father in the family garage. Among the Winston Cup stars racing today there are a handful of drivers who followed their fathers or older brothers into the sport such as Earnhardt, Dale Jarrett and Sterling Marlin.

Take Johnny Benson. Benson, the 1995 Busch Grand National champion now the driver of the Pennzoil Pontiac, grew up in a household where his father operated a family-owned race car parts business. Yet, despite his access to the sport, Benson didn't get started driving until he was 19.

"I wasn't sure if I wanted to race," Benson said. "I finally came to the point where an opportunity came to race. I started racing here and there. I didn't really make a career out of it until 1992–93."

To get a NASCAR Winston Cup competitors license, one need only be 16 years old and pass a physical examination. Physical requirements aside, NASCAR bases most of its decision on allowing someone to drive on their experience. New drivers will either have to pass a driving test conducted by NASCAR officials, or present proof that he or she has a fairly extensive background in stock car driving.

"Experience has a lot to do with it, " said Kevin Triplett, manager of communications for NASCAR. "We get resumes with past experience. We want to know where they've run before. As wide as we stretch and with as many divisions that we have somebody is usually aware of what the guy has done."

NASCAR's age minimum notwithstanding, few drivers in the modern era — past 1972 — have started in Winston Cup before their 18th birthday.

"You have to be very driven," said Chad Little, driver of the John Deere Motorsports Pontiac. "We've all started by at least 18 years old and it's not until we're 30 that we've had enough experience that we're making good money. Every driver is determined. It's more of a mental drive than a physical one, although to run up front you have to have a good physical make up. The further up front, the more it's important. It's not like other sports where you have to be extremely strong, or quick, or have a high vertical jump."

Physical fitness among drivers is a fairly new phenomenon. In the early years of the sport, the only concern was the horsepower under the hood. The drivers tended to be big, beefy men, according to Benny Parsons, the not-so-small 1973 Winston Cup champion turned ESPN broadcaster. There were some small men, however. Rex White, who stood five feet four inches tall drove a Chevrolet in the early '60s. Compared to the beefy Junior Johnson, a fellow Chevrolet driver at the time, White was a munchkin.

The men needed to be big because they had to wrestle the cars around the track. But the need for beef was eliminated in the early '80s, when power steering was introduced on the cars, Parsons said. "It's been one of the biggest aids."

"I think first it helps to have a physical ability," said Ned Jarrett, a two-time NASCAR champion, now an ESPN announcer. "That helps you to physically drive the car. You also have to have the right mental attitude. Having the right positive attitude that you're going to win. You've got to keep that attitude. You've got to keep yourself pumped up."

Fact is, mental preparedness and the ability to make split-second decisions is a cornerstone to being a great race car driver. Though some races go on for hours and hours, there isn't one moment when a driver can relax. No matter where they're running on the track, a driver's attention must be totally focused on what is happening in the race. One brief lapse and catastrophe can strike.

Even those drivers seemingly out of contention for the win must stay alert during a race in order to communicate how the car's reacting back to their crew members. Rest assured, the strenuous pace of driving combined with occasional overload of carbon monoxide may make a driver disoriented or dizzy, but they will never be bored.

"You've got to be 100% concentrated on what the car is doing. What the car is doing when it's behind certain cars. What it's doing in front of certain cars," Benson said. "Once the race starts it's pretty demanding."

Demanding is an understatement. Imagine driving 150 mph for five hours straight. No bathroom breaks, no chance of getting out of the car to stretch your legs. The only relief you get comes during the 20 seconds or so you're in the pits. Even then, you're trying to keep the car running, juggling water bottles and waiting for the car to slam to the ground signaling it's time to go. The only other break in the action will come during caution periods when another driver crashes. Then you'll be able to slow down, but still no getting out of the car. Heat is a factor. On a good day, the combination of outside weather and the heat generated by the 700-plus hp under the hood will bring the temperature inside the car well over 130 degrees.

On top of this all comes the stress and strain required for driving a 3,400-pound vehicle into the high banked turns of a track like Dover Downs International Speedway in Delaware. Worse yet is Bristol, where a lap around the half-mile track takes just 15 seconds to complete. Throughout the day, as a driver fights to keep the car going left into the turns, he's fighting the G-forces that would otherwise throw him out of the passenger-side window.

To that end, a majority of the drivers participate in cardiovascular and muscle building programs year round. In recent years, many teams have added in-house weightrooms designed to build the endurance of the drivers and crew members.

"The bottom line is there are 40 drivers every week out of thousands across the country who would love to do this," said Rick Mast, driver of the Remington Arms Thunderbird. "You want to get into Winston Cup. That's everybody's dream. Everybody who gets into a race car, that's where they want to go. They want to get to Winston Cup. Well, if you're lucky enough or good enough to get into Winston Cup, then that's pretty neat. But, what happens once you get here is that you get that nice, warm, fuzzy feeling for about 30 seconds. You say, 'Yeah, I'm a Winston Cup driver.' Then, all of a sudden, it goes back to the grassroots of your whole existence in racing and that is wanting to win races. You dwell on wanting to win and it eats at you if you don't win."

When the racing started a majority of the drivers came from the Southeast. North Carolina, South Carolina, Tennessee, Georgia and the other southern states were hotbeds for drivers. But as the sport has grown, more and more are coming from other areas of the country. Rusty Wallace and Ken Schrader are from Missouri; Dave Marcis and Dick Trickle hail from Wisconsin; Ricky Craven is from Maine and Ernie Irvan grew up in California. Gordon, a California native, came to NASCAR through Indiana.

Another common thread running through the best Winston Cup drivers is the ability to communicate with their teams. A driver's biggest asset is being able to tell the crew exactly what they're sensing in the car. Is it loose? Is it tight? How does the car change when running in a draft? While it's easy to toss these phrases around in a barroom conversation, understanding exactly what those statements mean to the seat of a driver's firesuit is altogether different. A driver not only needs to be able to explain how the car is handling, but should be able to pinpoint where any trouble may stem.

"You have to be able to get along with your crew," Baker said. "A guy has to be able to tell them what's going on. Most of them are mechanically inclined."

The ability to communicate, however, isn't limited to one's performance on the track. He or she also needs to be able to converse with the public and the media, in a way unlike any other sport. No matter what level of racing or style, race car drivers today must have the ability to serve the dual roles of driving and promoting their team. On and off the track the drivers of today serve as representatives for their sponsors.

Off-track demands of drivers are at an all-time high in part because of the increase in what sponsors are paying teams to be part of the sport, and in part because of an overall boom in the number of sponsors each team needs to placate. Just two decades ago, when sponsorship wasn't as critical as it is in the '90s, a driver's off-track responsibilities were limited to occasional appearances at local car dealers. However, now it's not unusual for a driver to make two or three appearances each week, year round.

"What life?," responds Geoff Bodine, driver and owner of the QVC Thunderbird. "Once you're in [the season opener at] Daytona, your life is over. It's owned by the racing gods."

Of course, as a driver and team owner, Bodine's downtime as a driver is filled with ownership duties. Still, he's also seen a dramatic increase in the off-track demands necessary as a driver.

"In 1982, shoot, you didn't sign autographs," Bodine said. "You didn't need to go anywhere. You had lots of time off. There was a whole lot less to do. I started off with Pontiac, there were a few things to do — golfing at Hilton Head. Now you just go, go and go."

No other sport can boast the connection between its participants and fans. The bond between race car drivers and their fans extends from the highest levels of Winston Cup to the smallest Saturday night short tracks around the country. Virtually every Saturday night race track allows the fans to go into the pit area following the event to mingle and talk with the drivers. That access to the drivers continues up through the ranks — there are some limits to contact as the stakes increase — to Winston Cup, where sponsors and companies involved in racing routinely parade groups of fans through the garage area before the races. It's the equivalent of fans being let into the locker room of the Chicago Bulls before game time, which, of course, would never happen.

Where baseball and football stars have been slammed for charging a fee for autographs, stock car drivers have taken pride in not doing so. (Yes, it's possible to have to pay to get into a show to see a driver, but it's not the same as charging fans for their actual signatures.)

Building on that fan-driver bond, however, is the role of sponsors, who partially fund the team in return for the ability to use the driver and the team for promotional purposes. As a result, drivers understand that for many of them, no sponsor means no racing. No surprise, fans buy into that thinking, and support the products being plastered on the side of the car.

"In the mid-'80s when consumer brands like Tide became more involved in racing, there became more pressure on the drivers to become spokespeople," said Mel Poole, vice president of Cotter Communications, a multifaceted public relations and marketing company based in North Carolina. "A company's investment 10 years ago may have been $500,000. That same company may have to put out $6 million for sponsorship today. Once the numbers started going up, sponsors started wanting to get full value for their $6 million."

Depending on their contracts, drivers will make anywhere between 20 and 50 appearances annually for their primary sponsor. Associate sponsors will demand fewer appearances. Driver appearances may be at corporate functions, local dealerships, autograph sessions and at track-side hospitality functions. Each contract also provides a fee for any appearance beyond the contractually stipulated number of outings.

Dale Jarrett, a two time winner of the Daytona 500 and the driver of the Ford Quality Care Ford owned by Robert Yates, said he'll make between 20 and 30 appearances for Ford in 1997. He'll make another 10 for the sponsors of his Busch Grand National team. He'll do 10 to 15 dates for associate sponsors of either his Winston Cup or Busch programs. And he'll turn up at about 20 Ford dealerships around the country during the season.

To get the most for their money, sponsors often hire folks like Poole, who operates StratCom, a division of Cotter Communications that educates drivers and team owners on the proper ways of distributing sponsors' messages.

"Drivers are frequently the key brand spokespeople for a lot of companies involved," Poole said. "While most drivers are trained to drive quickly, they're not trained to deal with the media. We give them the tools to deal with the media."

For between $2,000 and $5,000, StratCom and other similar companies will train drivers and company representatives on how to deal with the media. All too often, drivers will turn up in a victory lane interview spouting off each one of their sponsors in such manner that it seems like one long commercial. That's not what sponsors want, Poole said.

"A common misconception is that we counsel the driver to shoehorn the sponsor in there," Poole said. "We counsel them to only work the sponsor in there when they get the chance."

That's a long way from where the sport was 25 years ago when Parsons was champion.

"When I was driving, we did some appearances, but most were freebees," said Parsons. "You'd speak at the Kiwanis Club or something like that. Each town you went to someone might have you come and speak. You might have done 10 of those per year. Today there's so much demand on the drivers to make appearances and pay them. There are no freebees.

"There's no way in the world they would do it for free. There's also no way in the world a driver can do all the things he's asked to."

During the season, a Winston Cup driver can expect to be on the road at least four of seven days. Many take Monday off. Tuesday through Thursday will be spent dealing with either personal or racing business ventures. Depending on where the race is, they'll either fly out on Thursday night or Friday morning. They'll stay in hotel rooms arranged by the team manager, stay in rooms and drive rental cars paid for by the team owner. Friday and Saturday will be spent preparing for the race on Sunday. Immediately following the event they'll head home to start the process all over again.

An average driver will spend between 50 and 75 days promoting a sponsor's message away from the track, not including extra travel days necessary to get to those events. The top echelon of the driving ranks, however, may be out more than 100 days a year. Each race weekend takes up at least three full days of time, which spread over a 32-event season accounts for 96 days on the road, give or take a few extra for travel days to the west coast. 1995 Winston Cup champion Jeff Gordon estimates he'll spend 400 hours a year travelling in airplanes. Factoring in time spent doing commercials, shooting promotional photographs and conducting media interviews, a driver could spend 200 days a year away from home. The rest of the time, they're either at home, pursuing other business ventures such as licensing and merchandising, or they're in the shop.

"You're traveling, you're home a couple days a week. I've got a lot of appearances scheduled throughout the year," Bodine said. "I wouldn't do all of this unless I loved it. I certainly don't have to do this, I can do something else."

How much interaction there is between the driver and the team during the week all depends on the people involved and their commitment to the sport. There are several drivers who simply show up at the race track each week and go about their jobs. Others, who may be more mechanically inclined, may visit the race shop during the week when not out somewhere promoting their sponsors. For others such as Darrell Waltrip, Bodine and Ricky Rudd, who own their teams and drive, racing consumes their lives.

While there is a lot of glamor and notoriety involved with being a race car driver, the lifestyle does take a toll on families involved. It's no secret, there is a great stress level when a loved one has a job that can take their lives at any moment. Time spent alone on the road often intensifies those feelings. Many drivers bring their families along each weekend and they'll stay together in mobile homes in the infield.

"It's really difficult on the family side," said Little. "Not just for the driver but for the crew members. We're never home. It makes it hard for the wives and significant others."

Benson agrees: "In some cases it can be very hard. Most of us have motorhomes. We take our families with us. In some cases we see our families just as much as the average person."

They'll put their families and friends through such stress and strain because they are performing a job that for many started out as a hobby and became a full-time career.

According to Parsons, the difference between being a race car driver and any other career is that for many drivers, racing started out as a hobby. Over time, however, they've been able to turn that hobby into a fruitful venture.

"Their vocation is their hobby," he said. "About 90 percent of the people who work and draw a paycheck, if they had their druthers they would rather be doing something else."

Indeed, most drivers will say they're most at home when in the race car. In the past, Earnhardt has said that his blood pressure is at its lowest point when he's sitting in the race car, even to the point where he's near sleep.

Yet it's a job not without danger. Though racing deaths are at the lowest rates ever, they still occur. Neil Bonnett was the last driver to die in a Winston Cup car while practicing for the 1994 Daytona 500. Drivers rarely talk about the risk and when they do it's often in jest. Death notwithstanding, there is still potential for serious career-ending injury.

"I think about it very little," said Benson. "I think it's just as easy and more profitable to get hurt driving down the street from my house. These cars are all built really safe. We all know the risk going in. It makes it easier the younger you start. Kids don't have fear. It's a high risk sport, but I grew up in it."

It has been said often by many drivers that if they were afraid they wouldn't be good at what they do. There isn't enough time to be afraid and if they were, if only for a moment, they could lose focus and control of the race situation. Depending on the track, there are times when drivers are at the very edge of peak performance. At Talladega, for example, they are driving with the gas pedal to the floor. There is no more power to be had. When the cars are moving that fast the wrecks are spectacular and horrifying at the same time. Those not involved in such incidents usually are witness to a part and then have to spend the next several laps driving slowly past the wreckage while crews clean the track. With each passing lap, they're reminded of the danger.

"You have to be able to see something bad, to the point where it's almost like a nightmare, and jump back in," said Baker. "It's the ability to block out the bad stuff. You have to go right back into the racing mode."

Like other sports stars, drivers on the Winston Cup level are well paid. But with the exception of golf, stock car drivers are the last professional sports athletes whose level of pay is actually connected to their performance.

The sports world is filled with stories of stick-and-ball athletes cutting multimillion dollar, multi-year deals that have no actual ties to their future performance. Some of those deals, no doubt, have incentive bonuses for meeting or exceeding levels of play beyond a standard. But they do not have a clause that penalizes for poor performance. A baseball player making millions will get paid whether they're batting .200 or .500. Home runs or no home runs.

Conversely, a stock car driver's year-end tally is directly connected to his performance on the track. With few exceptions, drivers are paid a straight salary and a percentage of their prize money earnings. Depending on the driver and their level of experience, their base salary could range from a low of about $100,000 (newcomers) to a high of $2 million (Gordon). Most of the drivers usually running in the top 15 overall are paid $500,000 on up. That fee is paid out over the season, usually in a few large payments combined with bi-monthly checks. In addition to the up-front money, the driver shares race winnings with the team on a predetermined rate ranging from 35 percent to 50 percent.

There are some drivers, however, who work only on a percentage of the purse basis. Typically, drivers getting paid by a percentage of the prize winnings are getting a higher split and are usually those drivers without full-time Winston Cup rides.

It's also not unusual to have the sponsor foot a portion of the driver's salary. These types of deals are done to give the sponsor a direct financial connection with the driver — the thinking being, if the team and the driver split, the driver and sponsor would go elsewhere. The lawyers, however, often have the two contracts — the team with the sponsor and the sponsor with the driver — expire at the same time in order to prevent a messy driver-team-sponsor breakup.

Drivers can also cut deals with their team owners for a portion of any sponsorship fees which they were responsible for getting.

Outside of driving the car, there are also a handful of ways drivers can profit from their positions. Licensing and merchandising of their images will provide a healthy cash flow for an average driver and much larger for those like Gordon, Earnhardt and Wallace, the top-selling drivers. Generally speaking, the driver, team and sponsor equally split revenues generated from licensing projects, with an average team capable of earning between $300,000 and $1 million annually from such ventures. On average, a team/sponsor/driver will split 15 percent of the wholesale price of a souvenir, which amounts to about $2 a t-shirt. As the sport has grown some drivers, such as Earnhardt and Gordon to name just two, have taken the licensing into their own hands. Earnhardt-licensed products reportedly generate $40 million annually.

Autograph sessions and appearances are another lucrative venue for drivers to boost their income. Gordon and Earnhardt are said to charge upwards of $15,000 for a single two-hour autograph session, while middle-of-the-road drivers make between $4,500 and $6,500 for the same two-hour appearance. Of course, unknown drivers are in little demand and may command less money per outing.

According to *Forbes* magazine, in 1996 Earnhardt generated $10.5 million in income, with a majority of it derived from off-track ventures. On the other hand, Formula One champion Michael Schumacher earned $33 million in the same year, with most of it being his fee for driving.

Despite the potential for large salaries, the racing community is virtually void of the public contract negotiations that go on within the traditional sports. There are no outlandish contract demands, no trade requests, none of the antics found elsewhere — at least in the press.

Insiders say such bickering does indeed go on, though it's not done in the open and it's usually on a much smaller scale. Top drivers today have cadres of lawyers and managers to help them with contract negotiations. But there are no publicity-seeking agents similar to those that pervade football or baseball. In those sports, when an athlete isn't getting what he wants, the story conveniently makes it into the papers where the entire issue is hashed out for all to see.

The reasons for a lack of such activity with racers are rather simple. At any given time about 50 teams have intentions of running the entire season. Beyond that there may be another 20 teams tops planning to run part time. So it is, if a driver were to make a stink, his options for going elsewhere are fairly limited. And if they left before the season was out, it could be a year before another opportunity on the Winston Cup level came along.

For the most part, NASCAR drivers have been able to avoid the nasty incidents that have impacted other sports. Certainly, in the modern era there has been nothing on the level of Baltimore Orioles star Roberto Alomar's spitting in an umpire's face during the 1996 Major League Baseball playoffs or a player going after a fan.

This isn't to say stock car drivers are saints, far from it. There are occasional incidents of fisticuffs in the garage area after particularly bad accidents. And they are prone to the same marital problems that face the rest of the world. But, compared to other sports stars, those stories rarely make it into print. Fact is, only Geoff Bodine's friendship with Tanya Tucker a few years back was juicy enough to make it into the supermarket tabloid, *Star* magazine.

No doubt, NASCAR's controlling force as a sanctioning body helps limit and eliminate the hubbub from racing that surrounds other sports. Within NASCAR rules is a provision to fine if an action is found detrimental to the sport. If someone were to cause such a stir and cast a bad light on the sport, they'd likely be subject to a stern talk from NASCAR President Bill France, Jr. and possibly a fine.

"A lot of it is because NASCAR wouldn't allow it," said Clyde Booth, director of race operations for Mark Rypien Motorsports. "If they had a crewman or a driver go into the stands that would probably be the end of their career. "

The pressures on Winston Cup drivers to perform are at an all time high. More and more teams are announcing their intentions to race on the sport's premiere level every day, making it tougher for all of the teams involved. It's not unusual at the major Winston Cup events to have several big-budget teams go home because they failed to qualify for a race. Just a few years ago, the only teams failing to qualify were the underfunded also-rans, and no one was surprised at their failures.

While competitors usually understand the vagaries of a sport where making the race or not can come down to hundredths of a second, sponsors are not so accepting. They're spending millions to have their brand logos exposed to the fans in attendance and those watching at home on TV. So when a team fails to make a few races, sponsors get itchy, and drivers, unfortunately, are sent packing.

Because of the increased demand for peak performance, teams are less likely to take chances in the future on brand new drivers with limited experience. Instead, they'll rely on the tried-and-true breeding grounds for past driver finds.

Miller Brewing-backed Wallace believes the next generation of drivers is likely to follow the same path to Winston Cup as he did through the American Speed Association circuit, a stock car series that runs in the Midwest. It's the same series that spawned the careers of Mark Martin and the late Alan Kulwicki, the 1992 Winston Cup champion.

"The problem you're going to have," Waltrip said, "is that there are no sponsors and very few teams who are patient with a driver."

Waltrip said teams and sponsors need to understand that it takes time for a driver to learn and develop the skills required to be a challenger on the Winston Cup level, no matter what their previous experience. Doing so may mean not qualifying for an occasional race.

"It's difficult to get a sponsor to go along with a plan like that," Waltrip said. "Sponsors want it now. They're under the same gun as we are."

Future drivers need to go directly to Winston Cup and maybe skip over the Busch Grand National series, Waltrip said.

"You can put him in a Busch car and look at him there," Waltrip said. "But in all honesty, if you look back, very few drivers have graduated from Busch to Winston Cup and been successful. If you're going to go Winston Cup get in there and do it."

Benson, who was the 1995 Busch Grand National champion believes all newcomers are going to have to go through either the Busch series or ASA before stepping up to Winston Cup. "As a car owner, if you're looking at a driver, you're going to want someone with experience," Benson said. "I think there are only a few avenues to Winston Cup. I think the [NASCAR Craftsman] Truck Series is an avenue."

Back in 1991, Little ran 27 races for a family owned Winston Cup team. In the following years he drove for a few other owners without great success. Little then moved to the Busch series where he'd been a title contender in each successive season. Feeling he had gotten enough experience and having the right opportunity, he moved back to Winston Cup in 1997.

"Drivers are going to come from the series that give them the most experience to compete on the Winston Cup level," Little said. "Most of the drivers will come from Busch."

However, with more folks trying to make every race, it's going to be a lot harder for team owners to take a chance with new, less experienced drivers, he said.

Bodine, who broke into the series after a successful career as a NASCAR Modified driver in the Northeast, believes the next generation of drivers will have a direct connection to the drivers of today.

"A lot of them are going to come from the families of drivers already here," he said. "Earnhardt's, Jarrett's, my son. You're going to see a lot of the same names in this sport for a long while."

While Bodine admits the drivers of the future are going to need more experience, he does think there will be more openings available, simply because there are many more new teams coming into the sport.

"In the early '80s, there were no opportunities," he said. "I happened to be here at the right time. It was an era when there weren't any opportunities. Now there are new opportunities."

4

THE TEAMS

The Men and Money
Behind the Drivers

Got a spare $4–6 million? If so, you too could be a Winston Cup team owner.

Prior to the start of the 1997 season, 47 teams notified NASCAR they would attempt to run the entire Winston Cup season. Conservatively speaking, that represents expenditures of $188 million just on the annual cost of running those teams. Factor in a handful of part-time teams, and the Winston team costs could exceed $200 million a year.

One of the often overlooked factors in any driver's record of wins and losses is the team backing them up. The driver is the quarterback, if you will. The team, his offensive line, receivers and running backs. Behind each and every one of the drivers racing on Sunday stands 40 or more other people who in ways both small and large contribute to the driver's on-track efforts.

If football is a game of yards, racing is a sport of seconds — tenths of seconds. Often the difference between the team starting on the pole and the very last car in the field is measured in hundredths of seconds. With the cars so close, a team can make or break a driver.

In today's competitive racing marketplace, races are often won and lost in the pits, where team members will plot and execute racing strategy throughout the course of the event. But there's more to a team than those who show up at the track on Sunday. In addition to the folks working the pits on Sunday, many others at the race shop back home are building, painting, tuning cars so the following weekend the driver may have a moment of glory.

What separates the top teams and those running in the middle of the pack comes down to one thing: chemistry. The operations that are at the top of the field week in and week out are often those that have been together the longest. Each year a team is together, the stronger it gets. That relationship usually pays off on the track in wins.

The team concept has been part of stock car racing since its inception. However, comparing the teams of yesteryear to today's would be a little like comparing the plane the Wright brothers first flew at Kitty Hawk to the Space Shuttle. It's still flying, but there is no comparison. Today's teams are highly technical and finely tuned operations.

When moonshine runners started racing in the '40s, the drivers did most of the work on the cars themselves. During the day, drivers routinely tinkered with their cars to find ways to outrun the federal revenuers trying to shut down their illegal liquor operations. As a result, when they went to race they often went alone. Crew members were friends and fellow shadetree mechanics who lent a hand as a way to go racing. They were a rag-tag bunch at best.

Teams worked that way for the first few decades of the sport's existence. In the late '70s and early '80s, teams relied on very few full-time employees. For example, Larry McReynolds, crew chief for Goodwrench-backed driver Dale Earnhardt recalls breaking into Winston Cup racing in 1980 with a three-man team that attempted to run the entire season.

"A good crew chief," he said, "had to be a good mechanic. He didn't really have to be a good leader, because he only had two people following him."

Today, a basic team has about 40 people, though others have many more. Hendrick Motorsports, which fields cars for 1996 champion Terry Labonte, 1995 champion Jeff Gordon and Ricky Craven has nearly 200 employees. Felix Sabates who owns a three-car team with drivers Joe Nemechek, Wally Dallenbach and Robby Gordon has a team of 130. And Darrell Waltrip Motorsports counts 40 on its payroll.

The expansion in team size is a direct result of the increased level of competition — it's getting harder for teams to make the starting field — and because of the increased use of technology. When the competition level wasn't so strong, teams showing up at the track could often back into a race, albeit starting in the rear. Now good teams often go home. Put simply, there are too many teams for too few starting positions.

As the number of formidable competitors has grown, so too have the expenses of each team participating on the Winston Cup level. Sophistication in machining and development has forced teams to invest in high-tech equipment. Teams that once bought or leased engines from an outside supplier are now creating their own in-house engine operations. And competition among teams for talented people has pushed up the overall cost of operating a team.

"Right now," said Waltrip, "we're entering that era of technology, you've got to know how to run the machinery, the shock dynos. You've got to have people that are smart enough to do that. Our industry right now is kind of like the general business world was with automation 15 years ago. "

While no two teams are alike in their financial operations, the basic system is to have the sponsor dollars cover the annual cost of running a team. This includes payroll, driver's salary, travel costs, and any other incidental expenses. A team owner's profit is derived from his percentage of the race winnings, licensing and merchandising and any other outside revenue streams beyond the actual racing operation. For example, some of the major teams such as Hendrick Motorsports, Robert Yates Racing and Roush Racing make engines for other teams as a way to raise revenue.

The saying, "To make a small fortune start out with a big one," has been a staple in the team owner's joke repertoire for decades. And early on it was true. Sponsorship dollars in the late '70s and early '80s were just a sliver of what they are today. There's no denying money invested in racing could generate a better rate of return if invested in something more stable.

Today, team owners with front-running cars are able to make money, decent money measured in the millions. Those farther back in the pack, of course, have a tougher time, although with smart budgeting can still make money.

"You set down and see what you have to spend and you try not to spend it all," Waltrip said. "The thing is the payroll. The biggest item is the people cost."

A decade ago, a team could run competitively for $1 million a year. In 1990, it cost $2–$2.5 million to run with the leaders. Now, an investment of $4 million a year would be the minimum to run among the top 15 teams. The best operations are spending much more.

Hendrick Motorsports reportedly has an operating budget of $29 million annually. Of those costs, roughly $7 million is earmarked for each team with the balance spent on company-wide research and development.

Sabates, who called 1997 a rebuilding year for his racing operation, said he'll spend $19 million, or just over $6 million per team. Sponsorship won't cover it all, he said. The remainder will be paid out of his own pocket.

"I've been in it 11 years," Sabates said. "I've made money just about every year."

Between 40 percent and 50 percent of a team's overall annual operating budget goes to paying employees. However, the cost of finding and keeping good employees has skyrocketed as each new team has emerged. Where team members once would stay with one shop for a long time — no matter how the team was performing on the track — they're now willing to move around more.

"A lot of guys, we train them, they make $500 a week and then they leave," said Waltrip. "It's not only frustrating, it makes me mad . . . We've got guys who'll leave for $25 more a week."

Sabates has been slammed by other team owners for his willingness to pay high salaries. Still, he, too, is having to dig deeper to keep people.

"It's getting crazy for talent," Sabates said. One former Sabates staffer left because he got a $28,000 a year pay raise from another team. The employee brought the offer to Sabates who declined to match it. "If I did that everybody would be taking pot shots at me."

The average chassis or body shop mechanic makes about $800 a week or about $41,000 a year, with the pay range going from a low of $500 to a high of $1,500 a week. An average crew chief's pay is $150,000. Those crew chiefs on the highest levels of the sport are in the mid-$300,000 range annually.

All of those positions include two weeks or more vacation, health benefits and some of the higher levels — crew chiefs, team managers, etc. — have the use of company vehicles. There are also year-end bonuses. According to Waltrip, everyone on his team gets $2,500 at Christmas no matter how the team did during the season. Usually, a team owner will kick in 10 percent of all prize money to a fund that is split equally among team members.

Aside from payroll, a team owner's initial investment would be in cars (about 10 at $100,000 apiece), a team hauler/tractor to carry the cars and equipment to each race (about $300,000), tires ($500,000 to $600,000 a year) and the cost and maintenance of a race shop, preferably located somewhere near the Charlotte, NC., area.

Depending on where the race is and how the team performs, the cost of running each race is between $80,000 and $150,000. Obviously, a wreck will increase the overall cost of the weekend, while a win will dramatically lower the price tag. And starting in 1997, each team had to factor in two additional and costly trips west for races in Texas and California.

According to Sabates, his team's travel budget in 1997 is $680,000 not including the cost to run his planes or out of pocket trackside expenses.

Typically, a driver's salary makes up about 15 percent of the overall operating budget.

"I don't mind paying the drivers," Sabates said. "When the driver gets in the car, his life could be over in 30 seconds. If not, his career could be over."

Sabates attributes much of the soaring costs to suppliers who he believes overcharge NASCAR teams because they have something of a monopoly on the business, including hotels which triple their rates and parts manufacturers.

"We get gouged as a car owner," Sabates said. "Suppliers take advantage of us. [For crank shafts], you can go to a Chevy dealer and pay $800. A racing crank costs $3,500. Same thing with the transmissions. We're paying $6,000, there's only one guy making them. Tire bills are astronomic. NASCAR could have some control over that."

A team owner has three revenue streams to cover his costs and if they're smart, a profit. First and foremost, of course, is sponsorship dollars. Typical front running teams get $3 million to $6 million annually from their primary sponsor — those with the premium positions on the body panels. It's also possible to generate upwards of $2 million more in various associate sponsorship deals, which get less exposure.

The team also gets a portion of any prize money won by the driver. Usually, the team keeps 60 percent of the tally, with 10 percent then earmarked for a team-member bonus fund.

Nevertheless, since how a team will finish is a great unknown and something that is often affected by variables not under control of the team, owners generally don't figure on generating a lot of prize money.

Based on the standard 60 percent of prize money earned, Hendrick Motorsports would have collected an estimated $2.4 million of the $4,030,648 prize money earned by 1996 Winston Cup champion Labonte. Roush Racing would have gotten $1.1 million of the $1,887,396 earned by fifth-place finisher Martin. And Robert Yates Racing posted an estimated $1 million of the $1,683,313 of prize money from tenth place finisher Ernie Irvin.

A potentially vast area for generating revenues for the teams comes from souvenir sales. Generally, the team licenses outside companies to make products using their likeness and logos. In return, the team gets a percentage of the wholesale costs of the goods, which is split equally between the driver, team and sponsor. Like performance on the track, the level of souvenir sales is directly tied to the driver. A winning driver tends to sell much more product than those at the rear of the pack.

Top fan favorites such as Earnhardt, Gordon and Wallace sell millions of dollars worth of goods each year. No surprise, those drivers who aren't such fan favorites make considerably less, though can still generate between $300,000 and $500,000 in revenues for the team.

A smaller, though potential revenue stream for any team, is selling off old equipment to other teams in the same series or elsewhere. Under routine maintenance programs, good equipment is taken off the cars before it's worn out. Teams in local racing series needing seats or other parts can find them at about half the price through the Winston Cup teams. A team can make $150,000 in used parts sales alone.

"This is not a hobby," Sabates said.

Multi-Car Teams

Following the lead of Rick Hendrick, whose teams won the 1995 and 1996 Winston Cup championships, the term multi-car team became an industry buzzword. Hendrick, who years before had been chided for trying to run more than one team as a unit in the same series, has since been revered as a business genius.

The reasons for the multi-car team strategy are rather simple. For the most part, adding a second team is not as costly as building one from scratch. In fact, it's believed the additional cost is simply 1 1/2 times the cost of running the first team instead of doubling the expense.

Also, with more than one team, an owner gains seven more test dates for his operation. NASCAR limits all teams to just seven three-day tests at tracks the series runs on during the season. But with a second team, the entire operation then has 14 test sessions. As such, one team can test at one facility while the other is at another track, with the results of both shared between the two teams.

Adding a second team also increases the chances at profitability for the owner. Since in most cases he's not spending twice as much to include the extra team, though he's still collecting top-dollar sponsorship, there's more of a cushion built into the bottom line.

The top running teams have already gone to the multi-car format and others are threatening. Hendrick Motorsports (3 cars), Robert Yates Racing (2 cars), Roush Racing (3 cars), Richard Childress Racing (2 cars) and Team Sabco (3 cars) are already on board with the multi-car strategy.

At the shop, the teams are one big family, with the fabrication area building cars for each of the teams in the same fashion. The set up and final preparation, however, is done for the specific teams and done to meet each driver's specifications.

But the multi-car team approach is not for everybody. Many single-car teams maintain that the multi-car giants are making it tougher for the one-driver teams to survive, let alone thrive.

"These bigger teams are not only sucking up all the sponsors, but they're sucking up the help," said Waltrip. "By having multi-cars you've tripled your [sponsor] income but you don't triple your expenses."

Waltrip believes the multi-car teams are going to force prices for staffers up so high that there will eventually only be room for multi-car programs.

Yates, who fields cars for Irvan and Dale Jarrett, expanded to a two-car team in 1995 and has been very successful with the set up.

"When I'm sitting in the grandstand, I don't want to see multi-car teams," Yates said. "I like the opportunities [for single-car teams in NASCAR], that's healthy. I think that's the way it should be. But, if you want to keep up you'd better get like 'em."

"What fans want," counters Sabates, "is bumper-to-bumper racing. They don't care who the owner is. Owners don't win races, drivers do."

For all of the apparent benefits of a multi-car team, Yates said it's just as easy to double any problems that could occur within a team.

Ricky Rudd knows all too well what can happen when all the teams in a multi-car program are not working together. He drove for Hendrick Motorsports before forming his own team in 1994.

"When I was at Hendrick's, at one point there were four teams," Rudd recalled.

"They've come a long way with the multi-car concept. [When I was there] the drivers got along, but the crews and the teams in some ways went out of their way not to cooperate. Since I've been gone, I think it's been a slow process. They've taken it even further."

Wallace agrees. "I would caution anybody who thinks they can start a multi-car team and be successful. You've got to have all of your team members working in the same direction."

Adding new teams has become a trend in the same fashion that becoming a driver-owner took off following Alan Kulwicki's success in that role in 1992. The difference, however, is that the future direction of the sport is at stake with the boom in multi-car teams.

Critics of the multi-car system cite Indy car racing as an example of what the future may bear. Indeed, among the Indy car ranks, multi-car teams are the norm. Trouble is, the entire field is then owned by fewer people with more power, which is something NASCAR folks would like not to happen.

"I do go against monopolies," said Yates. "NASCAR will keep somebody from getting dominant."

Those not part of a multi-car team often say if NASCAR would change the rules regarding testing, some of the benefits of having more than one operation in house would be removed. However, that's not likely to totally upset the strength that the dominant multi-car operations have. That's because the power goes beyond testing. It extends to work in the shop and occasionally to team work on the track.

In fact, the 1997 Daytona 500 was a good example of how a multi-car team can work together. On the superspeedways drafting with other cars is the key to moving ahead. Throughout the event, crew chiefs often work out deals with each other to have their drivers work together to get toward the front. Once there, however, it's every driver for himself.

So it was, while running under caution with just five laps remaining in the 200-lap race, Gordon, in second place, radioed his Hendrick Motorsports stablemates, Labonte and Craven, who were in third and fourth respectively. Bill Elliott had the lead at the time and had been running good all day. But Gordon had made a deal with his Hendrick teammates to line up together to pass Elliott. Gordon made the pass, though the deal didn't work out exactly how he planned, as Labonte and Craven went high and he went low. Gordon won, trailed by Labonte and Craven.

For his part, Elliott, a single-car team owner and the only Ford running upfront, knew he was doomed.

"The way they were running, there was no stopping them," Elliott said afterward. "I was the cheese in the sandwich."

Though the odds are small that three teams from the same stable finish in order upfront, the Daytona did make a good argument for the multi-car team concept. According to Sabates, there is no greater example that the multi-car concept works. Hendrick had the top three and until a late lap crash took out 11 cars, Childress was in position to have his two drivers in the top 10, as was Yates.

Having more multi-car teams will have a profound impact on such independent drivers as Bodine, Rudd, and Dave Marcis, said Waltrip.

The multi-car teams "raise the bench mark at will," according to Waltrip. "It's going to run out the little guys like me, like Geoff. I don't think the fans are going to realize it, they're just watching cars on the track. They don't look at it the same way we in the sport would. I would be worried if I were NASCAR. You've got to have some slower guys for the faster guys to pass otherwise you don't have a show."

But not all of the single-car teams are taking the multi-car boom lying down. Already there's a move underfoot to have some of them work together in areas where information can be shared.

"The concept is good," said team owner Buch Mock. "The unique problem is that we are all trying to outrun each other. But there are some other things I think we can do jointly such as sharing in engineering and wind tunnel expense."

Mock said the goal was to share some of the common engineering information between two or three teams, including Rudd's.

"I think it just makes good business sense. My biggest challenge is keeping up with the sport. The sport is growing so fast. As expensive as it's become, I can make a few bad business decisions and bankrupt ourselves," Mock said. "If we make a bad choice on an engineering program or project, it doesn't cost me $400,000 and it doesn't cost him $400,000. It cost us each $200,000."

Banding together may be one way to keep some single-car teams from going under. Still, with sponsors demanding results quickly — primarily in the form of wins — some of the smaller, less well funded operations may go by the wayside.

"On one hand, I feel for the guys, the Marcis', why they do it, how they do it," Yates said. "It probably pays better than any regular job. They'll hang in until it doesn't pay like a regular job. If they wait too long, they may not get a job with [another] team. At some point, competition will move these guys out."

Finding Team Members

In the sport's beginning, it wasn't unusual for team members who came in as broom pushers to eventually make it as crew chiefs. They got their training on the job, watching over the shoulders of the more experienced mechanics and fabricators. Over time they moved up the ladder into full-fledged team positions.

Others broke in as weekend volunteers, who turned up each week at the raceway looking for work with any team that needed an extra pair of hands. Volunteer workers often found work with those teams that couldn't afford large full-time staffs.

While some folks are still able to break in at the bottom rung, a premium has now been placed on education and experience around race cars.

"It's like any business now," said Doug Hewitt, crew chief for Johnny Benson's Pennzoil Pontiac. "The computer age changes everything. We like to hire people that have been in racing in different aspects of their life. You need to have a certain level of intelligence to understand what's going on. It's a science; there are a lot of things going on that make a car go fast."

The sport has gotten so technology-oriented that every team has at least one or more trained engineers on staff — many with college degrees in their field.

Obviously, when searching for new people, teams like to cherry pick from other successful operations first. And since the number of front runners is limited, that makes getting good a tall order at times.

"There's still some pollination, some hiring from other teams," Yates said. "But you don't get the most popular guy around if you're hiring from other teams."

Likewise, team owners have had to dig deeper into their pockets to secure top-notch talent. It's not unusual for crew members to hopscotch around the Winston Cup garages looking for the best offers. It's also not unheard of for people to get offers significantly higher than their current salary levels.

The increasing number of new teams along with the expansion of many current Winston Cup operations has created a suction effect within the industry for new qualified players.

"A majority of them come out of the [car] dealerships," said Clyde Booth, director of race operations for Mark Rypien Motorsports. "Seems to be that they have the sense of urgency to get the job done. That and the fact that they can work neat and clean."

There does appear to be a changing of the guard among Winston Cup operations, as an influx of highly educated and race-track experienced crew members are stepping in to fill any vacancies.

"Believe it or not," Booth said, "The people we have are more intellectual than they were just five years ago. It's a lot different than it was a decade ago."

In another example of how the racing industry has moved closer to the regular business world, most teams are now signing contracts with their key people. A decade ago, a contract between a driver and a team was about the extent of legal paperwork in racing. Now, it's not unusual for the driver, crew chief, team manager and engineers to be locked in with a contract.

"You're forced to have a contract with everybody," said Sabates. "This sport has gotten kind of like a free agency."

The apparent lack of top notch people to go around has made some teams start searching for potential employees outside of the Winston Cup ranks. People working in the Indy car series, which is technology-driven racing, are often sought after. While the cars are much different from stock cars, the general principles of aerodynamics and speed are the same.

This isn't to say there aren't people trying to break in. Crew chiefs are flooded with résumés from folks trying to get into the sport. Pennzoil's Hewitt said he got 150 résumés alone from engineers during the 1996 season.

"You've just got to look in other racing ranks, the Busch racing ranks, the truck series, even local racing series," said Larry McReynolds, crew chief for Dale Earnhardt at Richard Childress Racing. "You can only circulate the ones in the realm of Winston Cup so long."

Because of the increased technological savvy needed to be a player in Winston Cup, several colleges in the South have created educational programs built around race-car engineering. A decade ago, the only engineer most Winston Cup teams came into contact with was usually on the staff of the automobile manufacturer.

"We're Indy cars with bodies," said Jeff Hammond, crew chief for Waltrip. "We're computer oriented. We've got engineers we would have never have thought about having. Five years ago, we wouldn't have had spots for them."

Getting in the door for those without engineering backgrounds is tougher today, though not out of reach for dedicated workers. The need for experience notwithstanding, team owners generally like the idea of bringing someone up through the ranks. But because of the competition, teams are no longer willing to take chances on new people in key slots — especially on the pit crew. There is no tried and true method of breaking into the sport, say insiders. Like most everything in the world, timing is everything.

"We look for a couple of things," said Dayne Pierantoni, team manager for Bahari Racing. "Obviously, they have to have the right skills. We'd like them to be a racer or something. We want them to have the racer's instinct, to have that desire to win. There are plenty of of machinists, but is he thinking about race cars or is he thinking about machining? Does he look like he'd be a good fit? Does he have the right personality or is he a renegade?"

Part-time positions also exist. Many teams fill out their weekend crews with people who have no full-time jobs with the race teams, though are paid for their weekend duties.

"A lot of the time it's done through résumés," Hammond said. "People come by and interview. You say the right thing, you're there at the right time, you may get lucky enough to get the job. It's not as easy as it used to be, but it's still possible."

Most of the time, however, jobs are filled quickly after they open. On race weekends, teams work side by side in the garage area. During breaks and down time they'll hang out together. If someone happens to mention they're interested in leaving or a crew chief has an opening, word spreads quickly through the garage area.

"Unlike corporate America, we interface with our competitors every week," said Pierantoni. "You don't advertise in the

Charlotte Observer for a mechanic or a fabricator. You put the
word out and you get people coming in."

The Players

Most racing teams are set up with an organizational chart
that's not all that much different from any other company with
a $4 million annual budget.

Ultimately, all paths eventually lead to the team owner, although in some cases the day-to-day operation is left up to a
general manager. The general manager guides the business functions of the team while the crew chief will oversee the mechanical side of the shop. Each portion of the shop is then broken
down into smaller units reporting to the shop foreman, who
then reports to the crew chief.

While titles and duties vary from team to team, here's sampling of the various team members likely to be found on a major
Winston Cup team:

Team manager: If a team has a strong, hands-on owner, the
next person down the organizational ladder will be called a team
manager. A team manager will deal with much of the day-to-day
business operations of the team. He'll interact with the sponsor,
the car manufacturers, NASCAR. He'll oversee hiring, maintenance, a show-car program, team transportation issues and any
future planning. He'll report directly to the team owner. Salary
range: $100,000–$200,000.

Crew Chief: The crew chief has a couple of key areas to control. He's got overall responsibility for the team's equipment and
personnel issues dealing with the construction of cars. He acts as
a team leader — a coach of sorts — in the shop and at the race
track. When he's at the track, the crew chief is the team's
spokesman to NASCAR. As such, any fines levied against the
team will be against him. He'll call the shots during the race,
schedule pit stops, motivate the team and plot strategy. He and
the team manager work out race-day staffing duties. The crew

chief reports directly to the team owner or general manager. Salary Range: $150,000–$250,000 with performance bonuses.

Chief Engine Builder: They oversee a team's engine building and maintenance program. They coordinate research and development, provide race and qualifying motors for each week and manage all members of the engine shop. They, too, report directly to the owner or general manager. Salary range: $100,000–$200,000.

Shop Foreman: Some teams may have a shop foreman for each area of the operation — chassis, body and fabrication. The foreman oversees the actual work on the cars and carries out necessary operations as set by the crew chief, to whom he reports. His main responsibility is assuring the cars get built and maintained each week. He is in charge when the crew chief is away. Salary range: $40,000–$60,000.

Mechanic: Mechanics essentially put the car together and repair them when damaged in wrecks. They'll mount shocks, steering components, wheels, axles and anything else that needs to be bolted on. Some teams will have specialized mechanics, who will only work on the front suspension or the rear suspension, as well as a couple of general workers. Salary range: $25,000 (no experience)–$50,000.

Fabricator: These shop employees will actually manufacture parts of the car from raw metal. Only the roof, rear decklid and hood of a Winston Cup car are stock. The rest is crafted by hand by a fabricator. Welding and metallurgy skills are necessary. Salary range: $25,000 (no experience)–$65,000.

Machinist: Like fabricators, machinists work with metal parts to refine them for racing applications. Machinists work in either the chassis shop or in the engine shop. Salary range: $40,000–$60,000.

Engineer: More and more teams are hiring engineers for various race shop duties. They'll evaluate the car's performance from an engineering standpoint. In the past, much of the work on cars was done by trial and error. Engineers bring a more structured approach to the development process. Salary range:$40,000–$125,000.

Gear/Transmission specialist: Oversees the team's transmission and gear assortment. Suggests gear-transmission combinations for specific tracks. Salary range: $40,000–$60,000.

Parts manager: Oversees team's inventory of spare parts, handles sales of used items. Salary range: $30,000–$45,000.

Scorer: Records the driver's position on the race track. Salary range: $100–$125 per race.

Non-staff race day tire changer: Changes tires during pit stops, maintains airguns and hoses on pit cart. Can change two tires in 20 seconds. Salary range: $100–$300, per race.

Non-staff jackman: Jacks car during pit stops and maintains the jacks. Salary range: $100–$300, per race.

Non-staff gasman: Dumps two cans of racing fuel into car during pit stops. Salary range: $100–$250, per race.

Full-time staffers who work as part of the weekend advance crew also receive a few thousand extra for that duty.

Life Inside

Want to be a Winston Cup team member? Plan on giving up most of your life, putting in long hours and living most of the year in hotels.

Working on a race team can be an exciting and excruciating experience at the same time. And it's not for everyone.

"It's kind of like getting an opportunity to go to the circus every day," Hammond said. "When it's going very good and you're successful, there's nothing more fun than racing. It's kind of like being in war games. You sit down with your driver and you go out and try to infiltrate the army next to you. A race track is the ultimate goal. You try to conquer it. If you do, you win."

Depending on their jobs with the team, some staffers can work as little as 40 hours a week and others, especially if the team isn't doing well, can work up to 100 hours a week.

On every team there are men who are part of the weekend brigade. Aside from their in-shop duties, they're part of the team's trackside crew. After working the first portion of the week in the shop, the advance team, or those part of the weekend crew, will be at the track when it opens on Friday. They'll work all weekend, including race day, and return to the shop on Monday.

On average, the weekend advance crew members will spend 110 or more nights on the road away from home.

Members of the weekend advance crew turn in the longest hours of any staffer on a race team. Despite a crew chief's best efforts there will be times during the season when they'll go several weeks straight without a day off. On race weekends, if the track opens at 6 a.m., they'll be there at 6 a.m. Also, they won't leave until NASCAR officials come around and kick them out, which is usually 12 hours later. They'll repeat the process right up until race day.

Those doing weekend duty tend to be younger and unmarried.

"We don't require [they not be married] but it helps," said Pierantoni. "It's just so tough when people have families. We have all three, single, married and married with kids . . . There have been many destroyed marriages in this sport."

The other part of the crew — those who work on the cars at the shop but do not attend races — will work Monday through Friday and occasionally on Saturday. And unless a car needs to be finished by the following week, they're likely to be watching the race from home.

"It's tough in that it's a demanding sport," Hammond said. "It's demanding from the time aspect. You can work endlessly. There's so much that can be done, so much that needs to be done. You can work yourself to death. It takes away from normal life."

Racing is different from other sports in that there are deadlines that must be met to keep the team on the track. Cars need to be completed for upcoming races. Past wrecks need to be repaired. General maintenance needs to be done elsewhere on other cars. It's not like baseball where an injured player is put on reserve and easily replaced. Though every team member gets at least two weeks of vacation, in-season vacations are unheard of. Most teams close down between Christmas and New Year's Day, giving every member at least one solid week off.

"If you want to work in Winston Cup you've got to be there every Sunday," Hammond said. "There again, that takes a unique breed of person. Most of them like and love the sport they're in."

Indeed, there are other easier ways to make money. But there are few other jobs that can provide the same level of excitement of that of a crew member. Completing a fast pit stop or figuring out what may be making a car skip a beat on the track delivers the same satisfaction an offensive lineman in football feels when he makes an opening in the defense that allows the running back to make a few extra yards on a carry.

Other than the crew chief, it's rare that the average fan will ever know the names of the other members on the team. There's little public glory for the person who changes a right rear tire. Yet that doesn't lessen their enthusiasm for the sport or their importance to the overall success of the team.

"We are actively looking for people who are committed," said Wallace, driver of the Penske South, Miller Brewing Thunderbird. "This is a tough, tough sport. We're looking for guys who are not married, without a lot of commitments. We look for guys who are clean and look good. We want guys who eat and breathe racing. It's not punch a time clock and go home and tend the garden."

If the a team member ever sat down with a calculator and divided his salary by the numbers of hours he works, the figure would come out rather small, according to Pierantoni. That begs the question, So why do it?

"Because they're racers," he said. "I don't know how else to explain it. They don't just like it, they love it."

5

RACE WEEKENDS
Life at the Racetrack

The truck drivers in Winston Cup racing are best compared to roadies working on concert tours around the country. In both professions, they're the first to come and the last to leave.

The truck driver is responsible for making sure the team hauler has all the proper gear and equipment necessary for the weekend's event. And he is responsible for getting the truck to the track on time.

To do so, he'll leave the race shop on either Wednesday or Thursday, depending where the race is being held. For the races at Sears Point or the new California Speedway, drivers will leave Charlotte on Monday.

With the exception of a few events — The Coca-Cola 600 and the Daytona 500 — the tracks open early on Friday morning to kick off the race weekend.

The team haulers line up outside the raceway before sunrise on Friday morning. Though times vary track by track, most tracks open at either 5 a.m. or 6 a.m. The truck drivers will usually have about an hour to maneuver the big-rigs into position within the Winston Cup garage area. The haulers are positioned in the garage in an order determined by the current points standings. The previous year's champion gets the first stall.

Unless it's a track they'll drive to, the weekend advance members of a race team will fly in on late Thursday night. They'll arrive on Friday morning when the garage area opens up for Winston Cup teams. The weekend crew usually consists of the driver, crew chief, engine builder, team manager and a chassis mechanic.

After the car and all the necessary equipment is unloaded, the teams will go through the first of many inspections that will occur before the weekend is over. During these first inspections, NASCAR focuses on the construction of the car and on such items as the fuel cell and the roll cage.

On all speedways there are rookies meetings held during the early hours, which will be followed by the draw for the qualifying order.

Following a complete inspection by NASCAR officials, which will include fitting templates, weight, height, and so on, the teams are ready for the first practice session on Friday, which gets underway at 9 a.m. and lasts two hours.

Generally, from 11 a.m. to 12:30 p.m., teams will make any final adjustments on the cars, refuel them, and take them through NASCAR's inspection process again.

Qualifying is held at 12:30 p.m. and based on the times recorded NASCAR will set the first 25 starters. Qualifying is usually followed by another practice session. Once practice is over, teams return to their hotel rooms and prepare for the next day.

The garage area usually opens between 7 a.m. and 8 a.m. on Saturday morning. Practice takes place from 9:30 to 10:30 a.m. At 11 a.m., another qualifying session is held for those teams attempting to better their times from Friday.

Saturday qualifiers, no matter what the speed, cannot improve their position above the 26th starting spot. Teams falling below 25 on Friday have the option of sticking with their Friday speeds or trying to run faster on Saturday. Often, second round qualifiers are limited to just a handful of teams and those are typically the ones at the very bottom of the list.

As with Friday, Saturday qualifiers are forced to go through NASCAR's inspection process before lining up for qualifying, which is scheduled shortly after the first practice session.

The hours after second-round qualifying are most often occupied with a support event. During this time, most teams will remove the engines they used to qualify and replace them with the race engine, built specifically for the track which they are running.

Winston cup teams will go over all parts of their cars and make any final adjustments before the last practice session held immediately following the support event.

The last practice, held late in the afternoon on Saturday, is called "happy hour" because cars run faster in the cool temperatures. Happy hour is the last time teams will be able to test any adjustments they may have made on the car and to put some hard laps on the race motor. Shortly after pracice ends, the Winston Cup garage will be closed and locked for the night.

Early Sunday morning, the weekend warriors, those crew members who fly in for race day only, will hop aboard chartered planes in Charlotte and head for the track. If the race is on the West Coast, they'll leave Saturday night.

The garage area usually opens at 6 a.m. Sunday morning, with preparation for the race beginning immediately. Their assigned pit areas on pit road are prepared for the race. Tires are laid out, each measured and its air pressure checked. Lug nuts are glued on with an adhesive. All air guns are checked and the jack is oiled.

In the garage area, each team will go through a series of checks and rechecks of every part on the car. The engine builder will re-tune and time the engine, wheel heights and weights will be adjusted, the oil filter will be changed and the brakes will be cleaned. Most teams work with a list of about three pages of items that will be done before the car heads out onto the track, ranging from checking the oil to waxing the car.

After they've completed their race-day preparations, the team will push the car to the fuel pumps to fill the tank and to NASCAR's inspection area where it will undergo its final pre-race inspection. From there the car is pushed onto the starting grid. Then crew members will plug in an electric heater in the oil tank to heat the motor oil. Warm oil helps motors produce more horsepower than cold oil. The heater is powered by a small gas generator which the crew brings to pit road.

Early on Sunday many of the drivers, their families and the crews will meet in the garage area for a pre-race religious service. All drivers and crew chiefs will also attend a mandatory meeting with NASCAR officials. If either misses the meeting, the driver will be forced to start the race at the end of the field — no matter where they qualified.

While the drivers and crew chiefs are meeting, team members are cleaning up their stalls in the garage area and around the team hauler. Once the car is pushed out to pit road, there is nothing else for them to do until race time. They'll spend these few hours in the team hauler, eating and getting changed into their race-day uniforms.

For a 12:30 p.m. race, driver introductions will begin around 11:30 a.m. Like the driver and crew chief meetings, driver introductions are mandatory. A driver missing the introductions without prior approval by NASCAR, will be sent to the rear of the field at the start of the race.

During the time between introductions and the start of the race, drivers and crews will make any final preparations necessary in the pit area. They'll mull around pit road until the race starts and then spring into action.

After the race, the teams head to their respective haulers in the garage area. If they've finished in the top three, they'll go to an area in the garage designated by NASCAR for post-race inspections. If not, they'll load up the hauler and set out for home.

The truck driver, of course, will be the last one out of the track. Because of traffic in the garage and around the facility, it's often difficult to maneuver the big rigs with the garage area full. Sometimes they'll wait until the hubbub dies down and then leave, often long after sundown.

The next day, they'll unload the car and start preparing for the following race. A few days later they'll repeat the entire process all over again.

6

PIT STOPS

High-Speed, High-Stakes Ballet

When it comes to race day, winning or losing ultimately comes down to two things: the driver and the crew.

The driver, of course, makes the in-race decisions about what line to take on the track, how much gas to give the car, when to use the brakes and overall driving strategy.

But those skills, and the benefits that may come along with them, may be washed away with one bad pit stop. It has been said before that races are won and lost in the pits. And with the differences between those teams at the top of the sport being virtually indistinguishable, winning races can come down to the race day pit crew. More importantly, the difference comes down to the execution of pit stops. Sometimes speed in the pits counts more than speed on the track.

Before the green flag falls starting an event, teams have already made such key decisions about springs, shocks, engines, spoiler angles and the like. However, on Sunday afternoon the focus turns to completing routine, in-race servicing as quickly as possible.

Pit stops are a fundamental part of stock car racing. At the very least, cars will need tires and gas in order to make it

500 laps at any track. Throughout an event cars will need further adjustments as the track surface and the air temperatures change. Also, windshields need cleaning and drivers need drinks.

That's where the pit crews step in. The very best of them can complete all of those tasks in less than 20 seconds. But it wasn't always that way. Early on, it would take nearly a minute or more to complete the same service that occurs today in less than half the time. As a result, it wasn't unusual for a team to lose a lap in the pits during a green-flag pit stop.

Part of the reason for the slower speeds was because of the equipment they used. Jacks used in the '60s and '70s weighed 80 lbs and took numerous pumps on the handle to completely lift the side of the car off the track. Tires were changed with four-prong wrenches instead of high-speed air guns. And early on cars had screw-on gas caps which required the gas man to twist them back on during stops.

"We used to come in and the stops were 50, 60 seconds long," said former driver now TNN broadcaster Buddy Baker. "In the early '70s, they were 40 and 50 seconds."

In 1960, Wood Brothers Racing, which now fields the Citgo-backed cars driven by Michael Waltrip, were the first to start actively working on reducing the amount of time a driver spent in the pits. Back then, it wasn't unusual for a team to waste 48 seconds in the pits just trying to change two tires and dumping gas in the car. With work, they were able to cut the time needed for a two-tire change down to just 25 seconds.

"All of a sudden people said this is like a Broadway play," Baker said, "if we orchestrate these steps we can go faster. If you watch these guys today it's almost like a ballet."

With the top teams so close in overall capabilities on the track, each spot gained in the pits is one less a driver will battle for in the field. Passing a car that is roughly equal in speed and handling could take a driver 30 laps to do on the track. But a good stop in the pits could gain a driver several positions without the risk of wrecking.

In its simplest terms a pit stop could be best compared to the execution of a good play in football. In football, for a running back to pick up a couple yards on the field, linemen need to block their opponents, a quarterback must make a smooth handoff, and each man must do a specific job as outlined by the playbook.

A pit stop is similar in that each of the seven men allowed over the wall and the other five that will contribute during the stop behind the wall, must execute their appointed duties. The driver, racing's equivalent to football's quarterback, must make a good handoff, which would consist of pulling the car into the pits and stopping in the right spot in the pit stall.

Pit strategy starts in the preparation of the pit area. Teams work from large pit boxes, which are wheeled out to pit road in the early morning hours of race day. The boxes contain the various computers and TV monitors the teams use as well as all of the necessary equipment for making in-race repairs. Also inside are the airtanks that will power the guns used to change lug nuts on the tires, the large pit board used to identify the pit area for the driver and the gas nozzles that will be attached to the gas cans used to fuel the cars.

During the initial set up of the pit area, one team member using brightly colored duct tape will make a large backwards L-shape in the center of the pit stall on pit road. The L is used as a target for the driver when entering the pits. The long side of the L will face the pit wall far enough away for the jackman to operate the jack without hitting the wall. The short end of the L is where the driver should stop. If he misses either mark it could make it difficult for the team to perform the necessary work.

When a team pits is up to the crew chief, who has examined the vagaries of the track in relation to tire wear and fuel mileage. In a perfect world, a tank of fuel will need refilling at roughly the same time the tires need to be changed. Most of the time that's not the case. At tracks such as Dover, tires tend to wear out before a car needs refueling. And at Daytona, cars need gas before tires.

Usually a team manager keeps track of fuel mileage during the race using a laptop computer with special racing software. As each lap goes by, the manager hits the keyboard recording the next lap. He'll advise the crew chief on mileage throughout the race.

Tire wear is usually determined during long practice sessions, although ultimately the driver can tell how the car is performing in the race. Also, as tires are taken off the car during the race, the team's tire specialist can tell how the Goodyear Eagles are holding up. No surprise, new tires will produce faster lap times.

"Normally, I'm trying to think way ahead," said Larry McReynolds, crew chief for Dale Earnhardt. "If we just pitted on lap 30, I'm thinking what if the caution comes out in 20 laps? What if this thing goes green all the way? I'm thinking of many different game plans if the what ifs come up. You've got to really think about the different what ifs that may happen."

A good crew chief is like a good football coach. A coach has to have the ability to assess the situation, taking into consideration where the team is on the field and how much time remains in the game. A crew chief faces the same hurdles. He must assess the performance of the car based on what the driver tells him and what the other teams are doing. He must then select the right "plays" for the pit crew.

Exactly what will occur during a pit stop is determined by race conditions and how the car is handling. If a stop must be made under green-flag conditions, where the rest of the field continues at top speed, a team may opt to just change two tires and add only one 11-gallon can of gas. If the stop is being made under caution, where the field is slowed and no one can advance their position without pitting, teams will go for a four-tire change and two cans of gas.

The decision will be made by the crew chief and executed by the team.

Here's what happens with a full-service pit stop:

Team members can jump over the wall when their driver reaches the adjacent pit stall. The driver will position the car as close to the taped L and will attempt to aim the car outward to be in position when exiting.

The jackman, front and rear tire changers, and front and rear tire carriers will run around to the right side of the car. As the jackman pumps the car up, the two tire changers will be loosening the lug nuts on the two tires. With the lug nuts off, the tire changer pulls the tire off of the spindle and throws it to the side. Immediately, the tire carriers will hand a new 75-pound tire to the changer, who will slip the tire onto the spindle. While the tire changers tighten the new lugs, the jackman lowers the car and races to the other side.

When the right side work is being done, the gasman and catch-can man begin refueling the car. Each can holds 11 gallons of Unocal race fuel, which weighs about 80 lbs. The nozzle system allows for the gas to rush from the can and into the fuel cell. While this is happening, the catch-can man is holding a small can to a rear overflow vent hose designed to allow excess air and fuel to escape the system during stops. After the first can is empty, a second gasman, who does not pass over the wall, hands a second can to the gasman. It takes about 10 seconds to completely empty a gas can.

Not usually allowed over the wall, but helping service the car is someone washing the windshield who often also gives the driver a drink. Those tasks are accomplished using squeegees attached to long poles and with a pole designed to hold two cups of water. In some extreme race conditions NASCAR will allow the windshield washer to jump over the wall to clean the windows.

Once the right side of the car is complete, the team runs to the left side of the vehicle. The jackman pumps up the car as the tire changers go to work. The front tire carrier will wipe any debris from the grill and the rear tire changer will make any necessary chassis adjustments.

The tire carriers will each get fresh tires from tire assistants who do not go over the wall. They'll either hand or roll the tire to the tire carrier who will help position the new tire on the spindle for the tire changer. Once the lug nuts are tightened, the jackman will drop the car, which is the driver's signal to go.

Unlike the average folks changing a tire on their family vehicles, pit crews rarely fumble for lug nuts. That's because in the hours leading up to the race, crew members will glue the lugs to the steel wheels using an adhesive. So it is, when the tire is mounted on the spindle, a tire changer is able to keep his high-speed air gun spinning at top speed and go from lug to lug.

Occasionally a lug nut will fall off, however. Tire changers carry spare lugs on their belts to replace any that may drop.

During the '90s, a premium has been placed on pit stop speed. That has forced teams to step up the overall fitness level of their pit crew members. Many progressive teams added in-house training rooms and have gone to the expense of having team trainers. In recent years, scheduled workouts have become just as important to the success of the team as testing race cars.

"We even have a doctor we work with," said McReynolds, "to help with hand-eye coordination that best fits [each crew member's] job. We have a work-out program, with a trainer, and he works with each guy on an individual basis."

The trainer, explained McReynolds, examined the physical mechanics necessary to perform each task on the pit crew. The trainer then created a special program for each member, based on their specific needs. For example, a tire changer may require more upper body strength than another position. If so, that person will have a program tuned to build that area of the body.

Top teams also try to practice pit stops at a minimum of once a week if not more.

When they don't practice pit stops the results are evident on the track. Just ask Ricky Rudd. In October 1996, Rudd won the AC Delco 400 at the North Carolina Motor Speedway. But it was a win that almost wasn't. During the race his team struggled in the pits to the point where he brought in crew members from other teams mid-race to help his chances on the track.

Rudd said a few days after the win he'd have to hire a consultant during the off season to help get the team's pit crew in shape. While they were good, he said, they were not on the level of the top teams.

"When we are on top of our game, it's like we are a good college team and they [Earnhardt, Gordon, Labonte] are a like a good pro team," Rudd said. "We've just got to step it up a little bit and the only way to do that is through training."

Rudd said he had the right people, but they were "not doing the procedures like some of these other teams that have gotten really high-tech, very sophisticated, and that are spending lots of time and money on their pit crews and doing things that we're not taking advantage of."

Today, virtually every pit stop made during a race is videotaped and reviewed either during the race or later on, much the way a football team reviews films of the past weekend's game to find flaws in their plays.

Just scan pit road while at the track or on television and you'll see a long rod hanging down over each pit. At the end of those rods is a tiny camera that captures the stop on a video deck housed in the pit box.

"Now you look at it and it looks like a bunch of fishing rods," McReynolds said of the pit road cameras. "A lot of it is monkey see, monkey do. People say, 'Hey, that will help our pit stops, too.' I'll take videos home of the race and I'll look closely when they show other team's pit stops."

"To go faster you need to go slower" is another of racing's often repeated phrases that carries a lot of weight. Drivers will often say having a better line on the track and a smooth driving style will lead to more speed than driving wildly and wide open. Pit stops are very much the same way. Each crew member needs to focus on doing his job smoothly and efficiently. And if each man does his own job, the overall time of the stop should be fast.

"Our sport has grown so competitive," McReynolds said. "If we can pass three cars by virtue of better pit stops, we're better off."

That's changing four tires, emptying two cans of gas, cleaning the windshield and giving the driver a drink, all in 20 seconds and with only seven people over the wall. Think about that the next time your local mechanic says it's going to take all day to change your oil.

THE POINTS

Making the Grade

NASCAR's points system has often been criticized by competitors and fans alike.

Critics question a system that allows a driver with only a few wins beat someone with more. The issue came to the forefront again in 1996, when Terry Labonte won the title, though had won two races during the season. During the 1996 campaign, Labonte's teammate Jeff Gordon had 10 wins, but finished second. Third-place finisher Dale Jarrett had four wins. And Rusty Wallace, the 1989 champion, had five wins, though finished seventh. How is it that a guy with more wins finishes second?

Easy.

NASCAR's system isn't based on wins alone. It's a system that takes into consideration a team's overall performance and benefits consistency over the course of the season.

The NASCAR Winston Cup points system was developed by Bob Latford in 1974 and instituted in 1975. Latford has been around racing since he was a kid selling programs in Daytona Beach, when the cars actually raced on the sand. Over the years he's worked in various public relations positions for tracks and teams. He currently produces a newsletter called *The Inside Line,* which is chock-full of historical and current racing data.

Latford's program has built-in incentives to award drivers extra points for leading races and leading the most laps. It's also designed not to give a race winner a dramatic advantage over the person finishing second or third.

When Latford created the system there were about five teams with a reasonable chance of winning every week. (In 1997, there are probably 20 teams capable of winning on any week.) In theory, the design of the points program is one that takes into consideration not only how a team does in the races it wins, but how it does in those it doesn't.

In fact, the top five finishers are only separated by five points, with those finishing six through 10 only four points apart. Just three points separate finishers 11 through the remainder of the field.

A driver can also generate five extra points for simply leading a lap. The driver who leads more laps than any other driver in the field gets an additional five bonus points for a maximum of 10 extra points in each race.

Latford instituted the points for leading laps and the most laps in any event as a benefit to those drivers who tended to go for the win at all costs, but who also occasionally ended up in a wreck in their efforts. Drivers such as Junior Johnson and Glenn (Fireball) Roberts were hard chargers who often risked everything in trying to win. Latford and NASCAR believed there should be some incentive for drivers who tried to win and sometimes came up short. Neither Johnson nor Roberts were Winston Cup champions.

Today the bonus points are significant because they encourage drivers to get to the front. Teams will adjust pit strategy to leave a driver on the track when they usually wouldn't. Also, they'll attempt to stay out in front longer to collect the extra bonus.

For instance, in 1992, during the last race of the season, Alan Kulwicki remained in the lead long enough to assure he'd collect the most-laps bonus. Those points assured him of winning that season's point title.

During the 1996 season, Gordon collected 170 bonus points. Labonte earned 130 and Jarrett, 110. Bonus points can make and have made the difference between someone being the champion and not.

Points are only awarded to drivers who start the race. The starting driver must complete one lap under green-flag racing conditions. He can be replaced by a relief driver, but all points will go toward a driver who started the event.

Any driver qualified to drive on the Winston Cup level can act as a relief driver, provided he has taken some practice laps at the track on a given race weekend. And any driver who started the event can serve as a relief driver for another starter who for whatever reason needs to get out of the car. A driver cannot collect points for more than one car in a race.

NASCAR prohibits a driver from getting out of his car to race in another event going on at the same time. If that were to occur, the driver would be stripped of any points gained in the first race.

If, at season's end, the points battle ends in a tie, the championship would go to the driver with the most wins. If that doesn't break the tie, the issue would be decided by the driver with the most second place finishes, thirds, fourths and so on until a winner is selected.

Car owners collect points in the same manner as the drivers. Owners collect points based on how the car finishes, no matter who is driving at the end of the race. Car owner points are used to determine starting positions if qualifying is canceled because of weather. Those points would also be used to settle a tie between two qualifiers turning in the same times. Owner points also come into play when using provisional starting positions.

Here's the way points are distributed:

place	points		place	points		place	points
1	=	175	15	=	118	29	=	76
2	=	170	16	=	115	30	=	73
3	=	165	17	=	112	31	=	70
4	=	160	18	=	109	32	=	67
5	=	155	19	=	106	33	=	64
6	=	150	20	=	103	34	=	61
7	=	146	21	=	100	35	=	58
8	=	142	22	=	97	36	=	55
9	=	138	23	=	94	37	=	52
10	=	134	24	=	91	38	=	49
11	=	130	25	=	88	39	=	46
12	=	127	26	=	85	40	=	43
13	=	124	27	=	82			
14	=	121	28	=	79			

8

THE SPONSORS

Getting More Bang for Your Buck

Corporate America has a unique relationship with stock car racing. Ask the average fan who pilots the Tide car, and they'll say Ricky Rudd. Jeff Gordon? No problem, that's DuPont. Dale Earnhardt? Nothing but Goodwrench Service.

The bond between teams and sponsors is unmistakable. Fans refer to teams by the corporate colors they carry. They're also able to name a driver's previous sponsor and often the one before that.

As such, it wouldn't be a stretch to say that next to television no other aspect of racing has had as great an impact on the overall growth and advancement of the sport as have the sponsors.

Through off-track marketing, sponsors such as Tide detergent and Kellogg's Corn Flakes have exposed millions of new fans to the sport who otherwise would never have come in contact with the excitement of racing. Also, credit for at least a portion of the boom in racing lies firmly with the sponsors, who, through in-store and on-air promotions, have expanded awareness of racing beyond traditional racing outlets.

While the concept of team sponsorship has been around since the early days of the sport, it wasn't until the early '70s — after the auto manufacturers stopped operating teams — that sponsorship became a real factor in racing. And then, the sponsorship didn't command the attention or dollars involved today.

The start of major sponsorship interest can be traced directly to R.J. Reynolds. Faced with the loss of television as an advertising venue, the tobacco giant turned to NASCAR.

R.J. Reynolds' decision to back NASCAR's premiere series in 1971, sent a signal to other non-automotive companies that racing provided a viable means of promoting their products. The rest, they say, is history.

Fact is, in today's climate, without a major sponsor most teams wouldn't be able to race at all. Just scan the Winston Cup roster. On any given weekend, a couple of unsponsored teams — teams trying to make it on their own bankroll — attempt to make the field with little success. Those unsponsored efforts that are able to make the starting field are rarely able to compete with the well-funded operations.

Conversely, those teams with the big buck sponsors — those nearing or at the $6 million range — tend to run up front. One of the most repeated adages in motorsports is "Money buys speed." Without a sponsor, there's not much speed to be had.

A primary sponsorship — one that gets the hood, rear quarterpanels and most of the car body — goes anywhere from $3 million to $6 million. Other companies pay anywhere from $150,000 to $1 million to become associate sponsors, which get them lesser placement on the cars, although still generate some attention for their products. Associate sponsors would be assigned such positions on the car as the rear deck lid, the short portion of the door in front of the rear wheel wheels, the roof pillars or the rear panels of the car. The larger the investment, of course, the larger the exposure.

Companies get involved in motorsports sponsorship for a number of reasons, although the predominant factor is the sport's ability to reach consumers. More important, they're trying to reach consumers who have already created a track record of being loyal to the products featured on the race cars. In fact, numerous studies have indicated that on average, 75 percent of

NASCAR fans are likely to purchase a product simply because the company participates in racing.

Few other mediums provide companies with so many ways to reach their targeted consumers.

The average attendance at a Winston Cup event was 180,260 people in 1996, up from 75,643 in 1985. On average, NASCAR draws more people at each event than football, baseball or basketball.

In addition to the number of people who attend races annually, sponsors also garner attention through television and print media exposure, both of which have grown dramatically in recent years.

"We did a lot of market research on this," said Bill Becker, manager of event marketing of the worldwide commercial and consumer products division of the John Deere Co. "Companies like Deere are always looking for the proper venue to help increase brand awareness and ways to create a bond between the company and its customers to sell more products."

John Deere, which spent the 1994 and 1995 seasons as a primary sponsor on Chad Little's NASCAR Busch Grand National series made the move to Winston Cup in 1997.

Before getting into stock car sponsorship, Deere looked into other forms of racing, explained Becker. After extensive research the company found that the audience composition of NASCAR was best for their overall company goals.

"This hit our customer base squarely," Becker said. "It's purely a business venture and we believe it makes good business sense."

While the company had been involved with various regional sports such as baseball and golf tournaments, its sponsorship of Little's Busch and Winston Cup programs marked the first national sponsorship the company has ever backed.

"This NASCAR business is on a global level," said Becker. "That helps us build a better bond with our partners."

Many advertisers and sponsors are the first to admit that what they're after is NASCAR's fairly strong audience demographics. According to various audience surveys, the median income of the NASCAR fan is $40,000 annually. About half of those fans have children, 65 percent of them own homes, 53 percent are professionals or managers, and 73 percent use credit cards.

Another deciding factor is that 38 percent of the audience is female, which is high for any sport. Females, long coveted by advertisers for their overall influence, if not control, of most household spending decisions, make up 32 percent of the fans of the National Basketball Association. About 28 percent of the NFL's audience is women, while Major League Baseball's crowd is about 23 percent female.

Almost half of NASCAR's fans attend six races or more. Most of them will drive an average of 200 miles to get to the races. And on average, they'll watch 18 events on television annually.

At the heart of any sponsorship deal is a desire to build sales of any given product. But while a direct correlation between increased sales and sponsorship is a bit difficult to track, there are other ways that companies use racing.

"A lot of studies have been done, particularly in NASCAR, where consumers are loyal to the brands on the sides of the cars," said Thomas Floyd, chief marketing officer for Pennzoil, which sponsors Johnny Benson on the Winston Cup series.

Indeed, sponsors usually get involved in racing to either increase consumer awareness of their products or to have a venue to boost employee morale and create goodwill with its customer base. Some, and perhaps the best, companies attempt to do all three with their sponsorship programs.

In general, those companies looking to boost their overall consumer visibility tend to go with the front-running name-driver teams. Of course, they're also willing to spend a little more for that exposure. Named drivers and quality teams usually run up front, therefore garnering more attention from the media and television coverage. Repeated mentions of the sponsor's name and image during print and television coverage help add to its overall awareness factors.

Those companies looking simply to boost internal morale may invest in a team that doesn't always run with the front of the pack, which will cost less than the front runners. While those teams won't generate the same amount of television or media mentions as those on the top level, they will provide something from which to build an employee awareness program around.

Surely, no one wants to be part of a losing effort. However, some companies, by going with smaller operations, are able to achieve their targeted goals with less of an up-front cash outlay than those wanting their teams in victory lane week in and week out.

Nevertheless, winning is the name of the game.

Pennzoil, for instance, uses racing to generate new retail and wholesale customers. The company sponsors teams on most of the major circuits and builds promotional campaigns that tie in both retailers and consumers. To that end, they'll create a sale event tied to a local race aimed at generating increased traffic at a local Pennzoil retailer.

The typical sponsorship deal includes a set figure for the overall package, say $5 million for the year. Within the contract there are likely to be several incentive bonuses covering such issues as top-10 finishes, top-fives, wins and championships. Each may range in price from tens of thousands to $500,000 for capturing the Winston Cup championship. Sponsors and teams may also agree to other incentive bonuses for such feats as winning the Pit Crew tournament, being named crew chief of the race, or even pole positions.

No surprise, the extra bonuses are built in as inducements to for the team to do better, but also because winning generates more attention for the team. A championship, for example, could generate millions of dollars worth of media mentions and endorsements that aren't included in most sponsorship projections.

Payments to teams are often made on a monthly basis, with a larger up-front check cut earlier in the season.

For their millions, a primary sponsor gets to dictate the overall color scheme, sponsor name placement on the car, team uniform specifics and the color and design of the team hauler. Most of these costs are borne by the sponsor, as well.

Sponsors also get some input into what companies are added to the car in associate positions. All sponsor contracts prohibit teams from soliciting companies that directly compete with the primary sponsor.

To assure brand exclusivity, many top-shelf sponsors have taken that matter into their own hands. Instead of simply turning the millions over to the team and leaving the team owner to find the other associate sponsors, many primary backers are now buying the rights to the entire car. A sponsor will pay a little more up front to the team, then turn around and sell the space on the car to associate sponsors to help recoup their original investment. This method can generate as much as half of the initial sponsorship cost and gives the sponsor virtually total control of its investment. As an example, Valvoline reportedly spends upwards of $5.5 million to back Mark Martin's Jack Roush-owned entry. However, through the sale of the space on the rear deck lid and the front of the rear wheel well the company is estimated to have made back $1.7 million.

Moreover, in doing business this way, the primary sponsor can then cut reciprocal deals that also help offset the original costs. For example, an auto parts company can sign up a battery manufacturer in the associate position. As part of their deal, the battery maker may agree to supply the parts store with cut-rate battery prices. The primary sponsor reduces its initial sponsor expense through the sale of associate positions and then creates a way to get parts for its stores at a lower rate.

Sponsors also get to use the driver's image in its promotions and licensing deals as well as access the driver and team managers for company outings and events. The usual sponsor-team contract includes provisions for several driver appearances at no cost and then includes a figure for additional appearances beyond the stated amount. Depending on the driver, each of those extra dates could run upwards of $20,000 plus expenses for the sponsor.

In addition to the direct investment in a team, the biggest sponsors will spend millions on products and promotions built around the team. These support costs are rarely discussed outside of the boardroom, although are perhaps just as important to the success of a sponsorship program as the team's performance on the track. The general rule of thumb is that for every dollar spent in direct sponsorship to the team, a company should spend one to two times its initial investment in additional promotional efforts. For example, a company spending $5 million to back a team could be spending another $5 to $10 million in other team-related support.

A big portion of the sponsor's involvement with a team is promoting itself and racing. All of the promotional products, commercials, advertisements and handouts mentioning the sponsor and the team are paid for by the sponsor. These costs are not included in the company's initial investment in the team. That includes producing the driver's cards for teams to hand out at trackside and driver appearances, hats, print advertising, in-store advertising, ads congratulating teams if they win, and pre-race hospitality functions. If sponsors want to get really fancy, they'll take on a race title sponsorship.

An average team, those running in the middle of the pack with a moderately popular driver will go though 100,000 drivers cards during a season at a cost of between $7,000 and $15,000. The big stars, such as Dale Earnhardt and Jeff Gordon will go through well over 300,000 cards in a season.

Hospitality functions at race facilities are one way sponsors attempt to please their current customer base, lure new clients and help build employee morale. For example, a sponsor may host a function tied to a race weekend in which they'll invite their regional sales team, their clients and any prospective customers. Attendees will get a ticket to the event, a chance to meet the driver, a pre-race pit tour, some sort of trinkets, food and drink. Though prices vary for each venue, the average cost for each guest paid by the sponsor is about $150, excluding a hat and program. (Tickets to the event make up nearly half of the total cost.) So a sponsor bringing 100 guests to a track, such as the Atlanta Motor Speedway, could be looking at spending $15,000 to start. Prices are higher for events such as the Daytona 500 at the Daytona International Speedway or the Brickyard 400 at the Indianapolis Motor Speedway.

Aside from large-group hospitality set ups, which usually take place in tents around the track, sponsors may kick in for a luxury suite at one of the tracks. While limited in number, the enclosed boxes offer sponsors a chance to wine and dine a smaller group of clients in an air-conditioned suite high above the track. These suites at the large facilities cost $25,000 excluding food, beverages and souvenirs for about 25 people. Costs for larger suites can reach $70,000.

So how much will a team hand out in the way of premium items for fans and customers? A lot. During the 1996 season, Pennzoil distributed 311,950 driver autograph cards — not all actually signed by Johnny Benson; 14,711 yellow hats; 1,008 hats pegged to the Brickyard 400; 4,007 credential holders; 51,500 pairs of ear plugs; 601 life-size cardboard standups of Benson; 5,665 posters of Benson; 159,330 small decals; 1,941 inflatable cars; 944 small umbrellas; 204 large umbrellas; 1,180 rain ponchos; 6,361 "Welcome Race Fans" banners and 24,950 3 x 5 postcards. All of these items were paid for by the company and all carried the Pennzoil logo.

Title sponsorship is another way for sponsors to generate visibility. Ever heard of the DieHard 500? The Daytona 500 by STP? The TranSouth Financial 500? How about the MBNA 500? All of these sponsors have paid to have their names associated with a Winston Cup race. Why? Because in exchange for their cash, they'll generate valuable customer name recognition through print, radio and television exposure. In addition, they'll also build in some hospitality functions at the race venue, which will help boost internal morale.

In addition to having their name in the title, a sponsor will get large corporate signage throughout the venue that would be highly visible to race attendees and the television cameras providing the coverage. Also, all coverage, be it print, radio and television, will make mention of the sponsors name in describing the race. "We're back at the DieHard 500 and . . ." a TV announcer will say over and over during the four-hour telecast.

Prices vary depending on the size of venue — bigger tracks that lure more fans, of course, cost more — though for anywhere from a few hundred thousand dollars to nearly a million, a sponsor can immediately get their name in front of potential customers. In 1996, the Atlanta Motor Speedway sold the title sponsor rights to its March 1997 Winston Cup event as part of a three-year deal. The first year of the package cost of $650,000 with the price tag escalating to $750,000 in 1999.

Such packages usually guarantee the sponsor's name be printed on all programs, ticket stubs, brochures and any other handouts regarding the race. Sponsors will also get access to a block of tickets to the main event, as well as any other supporting races held during the same weekend.

Companies taking title sponsorship during a race are also likely to spend heavily on commercial time during the telecast to help support the coverage. Here, too, the costs could run into the hundreds of thousands of dollars.

The numbers do appear a bit steep. But by all indications the promotional opportunities generated for the investment are well worth the return. In 1996, the average Winston Cup race title sponsor was mentioned 80 times on air valued at $1,253,900, according to *The Sponsors Report*. That's up from 45 mentions valued at $843,000 in 1995.

Aside from the promotional handouts, team sponsors can significantly increase their in-race exposure by signing up for in-car camera coverage. They'll have to pay, of course, somewhere in the neighborhood of $18,500 per race, with no guarantees. If there's a technical glitch with the in-car system, the network airing the race will give the sponsor a free ride in another race. If the driver wrecks early and is out of the race, there are no refunds.

In-car cameras can also be used as a way to generate some, albeit minor, revenue for the team. Depending on who has control of the vehicle — the team or the sponsor — that company will go out and solicit sponsors for the small panel on the dashboard visible when the in-car camera is on. Getting that position on the dash may also be used as an inducement to get a company to sign on as an associate sponsor.

Corporations involved in racing are also urged to hand out free samples of their products at race venues — for a price. At larger facilities — Atlanta, Talladega, Daytona, etc.—the cost, not including payments to the people actually handing out the items, is between $8,000 and $10,000.

Sponsors also want to make sure their name and the team they're backing is mentioned by the media. To do so, they'll spend between $75,000 and $100,000 annually on a public relations program for the team. That fee includes having a representative at every race track to promote the team through print, radio and television interviews. A typical public relations program also includes press kits, including team information, photographs and other miscellaneous details as well as occasional mailers sent out to reporters to remind them of the team's activities.

In addition to the public relations efforts, sponsors often support their teams with show car programs. The operations provide race cars — either cars that have been used in race situations or exact duplicates — which are sent around the country to dealers, distributors or car shows. The goal is to further associate the sponsor's name with consumers and racing.

Likewise, the show cars are used by stores and dealers as a way to build customer traffic. Show cars can be a big draw. It's not often that fans can get a chance to see a real stock car up close and that's exactly what a show car program can do.

However, such programs aren't free. Teams and sponsors can approach a show car plan by either operating it themselves or through an outside company that runs such plans. An outside company will charge between $75,000 and $100,000 annually to operate a show car program. An internally run show car operation costs a bit less.

Ultimately, the sponsor is in control of the program and coordinates when and where the cars should be. In virtually all cases, the sponsor charges the dealer or branch managers a fee to have the show car delivered. While those costs vary, the average show car visit costs about $3,000 to the store owner, who, if all goes well, will be able to make up the fee through additional sales generated by having the car there. If the sponsor has budgeted the program correctly, there is a potential to generate some revenue from it, but not much.

Aside from increased corporate awareness and in-store sales, sponsors can also generate revenues from its efforts through souvenir and collectible sales. In most situations, the team, sponsor and driver license their names and likenesses to outside companies which then create products that are sold to consumers. The team, sponsor and driver then share equally the revenues culled from those licenses.

A mid-level team/sponsor/driver combination can look to generate $100,000 annually from licenses to die-cast car makers alone, according to Fred Wagenhauls, president of Action Performance Companies, a leading collectibles manufacturer. That same mid-level team can also generate between $250,000 and $300,000 from licenses of apparel — jackets, caps, t-shirts — and other team related souvenirs.

Some companies, however, are looking to be associated with racing without full team sponsorship. Those companies typically turn to sponsorships that make them the official (add any name here) of NASCAR. Busch Beer, Champion Spark Plugs, Goody's Headache Powders, Gatorade, etc. have all paid to be part of Winston Cup racing. For a fee, companies sign on to be the official and exclusive manufacturer of any given product included with NASCAR.

Western Auto, which sponsors Darrell Waltrip Motorsports to the tune of $5 million-plus a year, also kicks in $100,000 annually to sponsor a mechanic of the race award.

In 1996, DieHard Batteries was paying about $400,000 a year to be the official battery supplier to NASCAR. In addition to the cash payment, DieHard supplied batteries to each of the teams in the garage area, provided trackside technical assistance and sponsored the DieHard Hard Charger award for the teams. In return, each of the teams was required to carry a DieHard sticker on their cars in a spot designated by NASCAR.

Another is Stant, a company that makes radiator caps. Stant provides its product free to competitors. It also backs a contingency bonus plan worth about $64,000 for the season that for each race pays the first driver to cross the finish line with a Stant sticker $900, it pays the 10th place finisher with a sticker $700 and it pays the 20th place finisher $400. The company will give out more than 2,100 radiator caps during the season, according to Tom Roberts, who handles the company's trackside marketing efforts. In addition to the company's bonus plan and product commitment, it is also paying a fee to NASCAR to be part of the family.

"When they go dealing business to business with the largest auto parts chains," Roberts said, "they're able to say, 'We're involved with NASCAR.' It's something they take great pride in being a part of. And they're spending at a level they can justify."

In fact, each of the stickers appearing behind the front wheel wells is there because the companies are part of NASCAR's official list of sponsors. To take part in the post-race awards, such as the Hard Charger, or the Goody's Headache Award, a team must be carrying the decals. There are only a handful of decals that NASCAR demands be carried on the car — they strongly encourage teams to carry others. Those that NASCAR mandates can be seen on the two clean cars now on the circuit: Mark Martin's Valvoline-sponsored Thunderbirds and Johnny Benson's Pennzoil-backed Pontiacs. In these cases, the sponsor doesn't want their message being diluted by the vast array of stickers. However, in return, those companies usually agree to provide any cash awards a team would have won during the season had they carried a particular sponsor's decal.

Despite all of the media and fan attention, being a sponsor may actually be the biggest crapshoot in the business world. The dollars invested are huge and there are few solid ways to track the investment.

"If you do specific promotional programs tied to the team you'll be able to see [sales changes]," said Paul Mecca, director of racing for the Exide Corporation, which sponsors Jeff Burton on the Winston Cup level and Chuck Bown in the NASCAR Craftsman Truck Series. "It's a difficult thing to do especially if you don't have a program to go and measure it."

John Deere's Becker agrees. After two years of sponsoring Little on the Busch series the company is looking at several ways to measure whether the sponsorship package has had any direct impact on the bottom line. "We're looking into different research methodology," he said.

So far the best measure available for sponsors to judge the impact of their involvement in racing is *The Sponsors Report*, a newsletter that tracks on-air exposure for sponsors during racing telecasts.

Researchers for *The Sponsors Report* count all clear images of each car during the race coverage. They then compare that tally to what an equivalent amount of commercial time during the race telecasts would have cost to come up with an estimated value of the exposure.

During the 1996 season, Martin generated the most on-air sponsor mentions of any Winston Cup team with the equivalent of 12 hours and 40 minutes of air time for his backer Valvoline, according to *The Sponsors Report*. That time was valued at $29.1 million, which is considerably more than the reported $5.5 million in direct sponsorship the company is giving the team. In 1995, Martin was the top dog with 13 hours and 41 minutes valued at $33.5 million.

For 1996, DuPont-backed Jeff Gordon generated 14 hours and 15 seconds of exposure worth $27.7 million. Budweiser-backed Ken Schrader was third overall with 10 hours and 57 minutes of exposure worth $24.3 million.

However, if a team doesn't fare well or isn't a typical front-runner able to generate tons of publicity, the figures may not be so staggering. In 1996, when Terry Labonte won the championship, he generated $12 million in on-air mentions for his sponsor Kellogg's Corn Flakes, which is less than half of what Martin generated for Valvoline on the way to his No. 6 overall finish.

Some of the difference between Martin and Labonte can be attributed to Valvoline's decision to be a heavy user of in-car cameras. The company uses the tool in virtually every race.

According to Pennzoil's Floyd, the company is shooting for a four-to-one return on its investment in the way of on-air mentions. "If I spend $2, I want to get $8 in mentions."

In 1996, Pennzoil was on air for two hours, 44 minutes and 49 seconds worth $8,761,000 in commercial value. Pennzoil driver Benson was mentioned 175 times during the season, which is just three shy of No. 5 finisher Dale Jarrett. What *The Sponsors Report* doesn't take into consideration are local television mentions and appearances on racing interview programs such as TNN's "Inside NASCAR" or ESPN's "RPM 2 Night," where a driver can be on the air for several minutes.

Floyd admits getting a handle on increased sales resulting from the sponsorship isn't easy. They do know, however, how fans can negatively react when the company decides not to sponsor a team they've been associated with in the past.

"That's a tough one," Floyd said. "It's almost like measuring more advertising. We do know various racing activities have given more exposure to our products."

Additional exposure, he said, results in preferable placement for Pennzoil products in retailers stores and new accounts for the company's products. It's also a great device to help cement new business deals.

"We use racing sometimes to help develop partnerships," Floyd said, "not only with customers but with business relationships. Something about racing has a lot of mystique. People like to watch it. I don't know what it is, but there's some level of excitement you can see in the crowd."

That excitement has translated into new companies becoming part of NASCAR. A total of 523 companies were mentioned or visible on air during the 1991 season, according to *The Sponsors Report*. In 1996, that figure jumped 32 percent to 689 sponsors.

Not bad at all for a sport that had only a handful of big-league sponsors just 25 years ago.

9

TELEVISION

Bringing Racing to America's Living Room

Hands down, live television coverage of racing has been one of the driving forces behind the growth of NASCAR, and maybe the most important.

The marriage of motorsports and live television is, perhaps, a bond made in heaven for all parties involved. Few sports have thrived the way racing did once it was recognized as a legitimate television sport.

Likewise, television has thrived by offering motorsports programming to the growing legions of fans.

NASCAR ran its first race in what's now known as the Winston Cup series in 1949. However, television didn't become a part of the Winston Cup landscape until nearly two decades later.

For many years, TV executives considered the sport nothing more than something "rednecks" and "bubbas" did on weekends. It was decidedly too southern in nature to be put on national television alongside such sports as baseball and football, they argued.

"It was primarily on [ABC's] 'Wide World of Sports' stuck between arm wrestling and cliff diving," said Benny Parsons, the 1973 Winston Cup champ now part of ESPN's broadcasting team.

The first national television coverage of a NASCAR event of any kind occurred in 1960 when CBS offered viewers a two-hour tape delayed package of the qualifying races for the Daytona 500. The following year, ABC aired a portion of the Firecracker 250 from Daytona during a "Wide World of Sports" telecast.

Outside of a few taped bits of racing action, television didn't get on board with racing in any major way until much later.

"The first major change was the 1979 race at Daytona," said Ken Squier, a veteran broadcaster who works for CBS, TBS and others. "That was the first time a network [CBS] was willing to gamble that this colloquial sport could stand up for five hours."

CBS has been televising the Daytona 500 ever since. Today, the Daytona 500 stands as the highest rated race of any kind airing on any television network in the United States. The race is seen annually in more than 8.5 million television homes, according to Nielsen Media Research, which measures television viewing. Its ratings are rivaled only by the Indianapolis 500.

"There was nothing," said Ned Jarrett, a two-time Winston Cup champion who now works for TNN and ESPN. "No live, just some highlight-type of shows; it was nothing to compare with today."

Despite CBS' interest in Daytona, few other networks were willing to jump on the racing bandwagon. For the next few years, networks picked up only a handful of races each season.

Televising races posed a few problems for networks. Aside from the perceived regionality of the sport, races just took too long to complete. Typically, most races last five hours or more, which takes up a huge chunk of a network's Sunday afternoon schedule. Also, networks have to convince their affiliates — the stations that deliver the network's signals to your home — to carry the events it offers for broadcast. While this isn't tough with stations in the south, where racing was based, getting a station in the north to sign on for the telecast was more difficult.

Getting networks and stations on board wasn't easy in the early days of racing. The sport didn't have nearly the media following or general hype it has today, so network executives were slow to believe that folks would watch — and watch for five hours. And without the print media attention it generates today, broadcasters weren't sure what to make of racing.

The first weekly magazine show that included racing updates and information was "MotorWeek Illustrated," which debuted in late 1981 and aired on Saturday nights for five seasons on cable's TBS.

Racing coverage got a technical boost in 1983 when CBS introduced the in-car camera in a vehicle driven by Cale Yarborough. Previously, television consisted of images of cars simply circling the track with the announcers trying to convey what was going on inside the cars. The first in-car cameras were stationary and provided one view from the back seat looking forward through the windshield. However, the technology provided the view from the driver's perspective, which until then had never before been seen.

"Those cameras took stock car racing from a reality sport to a fantasy sport," said Squier. "Prior to that, stock car racing on television was pretty much regarded as something we all did. We all drove a car, big deal, we could do that on the Long Island Expressway. They [the cars] never looked as fast as they were and except for those sensational moments, there was no way to capture the subtlety of the sport."

However, five years after the first heavy in-car cameras were introduced, television networks started working with the tiny "lipstick" cameras similar to those in place today. The smaller cameras, which are literally the size of a lipstick case, opened up a whole new world for broadcasters wrestling with the issue of how best to translate the excitement of racing to the home viewer. While the first generation of in-car cameras were limited in placement to the rear portion of the car, the lipstick cameras could go virtually anywhere such as in bumpers, on roofs, or on the dashboard aimed at the drivers.

According to Squier, the fantasy sports are the ones in which viewers sit at home and believe that if things were different, they, too, could be a participant. "It's like watching boxing, and seeing a guy get hit," he said. "Then you say to yourself, he should have stepped to the left. I never would have been hit. What a dummy he is.

"Along came the in-car camera and it changed the perception of racing," Squier said. "The viewers were riding a 200 mph tight rope. They truly saw how fast [the cars] were going and how close where they were. In a period of a few years, a lot of people were saying 'Geez, all he had to do . . .' "

The in-car cameras raised the bar for all producers of race telecasts, said Squier.

Aside from the coverage on CBS and ABC, racing got very little exposure until the mid 1980s, when ESPN, then an upstart cable network devoted to sports programming, debuted. Like any network, ESPN was after good sports programming which was readily available at reasonable prices.

In the '80s, stock car racing fit the bill. Because the popularity had yet to take off, television rights to some races could be had for less than $100,000. In some cases, TV rights went for $50,000 per event. Because racing ate up a lot of time and was cheap, ESPN decided to make it a staple of its program lineup.

Then in 1991, cable's The Nashville Network, which offered programming with a country music theme as the back drop, decided to take advantage of the built-in fan base for the country lifestyle and auto racing. The network went on a buying spree and, by paying rights fees that were in some case five times the current rate, picked up about five Winston Cup events. Along with the Winston Cup rights, TNN bought the rights to all of the stand-alone Busch series events that until then had been televised on a scatter shot basis.

The cable networks realized almost overnight that the telecasts lured new viewers to their networks who had a hearty appetite for racing programming. More important, the networks were also able to attract a new group of advertisers, many who had previously not bought air time on those networks. In the early years of TNN's involvement in televising races, the network generated an additional $10 million in advertising dollars from sources that didn't buy time on the network before racing.

"Cable showing the world what Winston Cup was, helped show the world what NASCAR was," said Patti Wheeler, president of World Sports Enterprises, which produces racing events and programs for TNN, CBS and TBS. "People were just not aware of all the great drama, the personality and the fun of racing."

In the three decades, the sport has gone from having just a few hours of coverage each year to several hundred annually today.

Race fans scanning the television dial today can pick from live and taped events, specific shows geared to various aspects of motorsports, and call-in shows designed to let viewers talk with their favorite drivers. Moreover, there's Speedvision, an entire cable network devoted to covering motorsports, be it automobiles, boats or planes.

Television, according to Parsons, helped bring the sport where it is today.

"It increased the demand for tickets," Parsons said. "People saw it on TV and said, 'Wow, I want to see that in person.' It gave sponsors much more added value than just the people in the grandstands."

"TV and NASCAR have grown hand in hand," said Wheeler. "It's really hard to distinguish who did what to whom; they were really together."

When it comes to television, racing differs from other sports in that it's up to each track to negotiate its own TV rights package with a broadcast (CBS, ABC, NBC, FOX) or cable network (TNN, ESPN, TBS, Speedvision). For comparison, all of the major sports leagues in the country handle the television rights as a group.

According to David Hall, who heads up TNN for CBS Cable, when the network first got started in racing it was paying in the neighborhood of $200,000 for events at Phoenix International Raceway and The North Carolina Motor Speedway.

But as popularity of the sport grew, so too, has the cost of doing business.

Prior to 1997, TNN had been paying in the neighborhood of $567,000 for the annual July race at the New Hampshire International Speedway. However, when the track picked up a second race scheduled for September 1997, the rights fees soared 400 percent, according to Hall.

TNN beat out the other networks bidding for the event by agreeing to spend just over $2 million for the rights to air the race.

"NASCAR has shown growth," said David Kenin, the former president of CBS Sports. "It has shown ratings stability. It's advertiser friendly. In a cluttered environment it's a genuine program. I think it is a strong and compelling viewing alternative. If you're sitting by a television set it leaps out at you."

Under Kenin's leadership, CBS went on a buying rampage and made NASCAR's Winston Cup and Craftsman Truck Series races part of its programming mix.

The network also renewed its rights to the Daytona 500 and a package of other races at tracks owned by the International Speedway Corporation, a sister company to NASCAR. Under the terms of the new deal, CBS pays about $20 million annually for a package that previously cost $8 million.

Roughly 25 percent of the rights fees networks pay track owners to televise the events goes directly to the race purse. Another 10 percent goes to NASCAR. And the remainder is income to the track owner.

Using the 1996 Jiffy Lube 300 at the New Hampshire International Speedway as an example, the rights fee TNN paid to carry the race was $567,500. Of that, $141,875 went to the purse, which totalled $1,564,783. NASCAR's cut of the rights fee was an estimated $56,700.

While the rights fees numbers appear steep, they're a far cry from the hundreds of millions networks pay each year to televise such sports as the National Football League, Major League Baseball, the NBA or the National Hockey League.

The difference is, in part, because of the lower audience numbers. Still, the viewership numbers are growing.

Nearly six million spectators turned out for a race on NASCAR's Winston Cup Circuit in 1996, making it the fastest-growing sport in America.

Richard Petty, known as "The King," is one of the most enduring personalities in all of professional stock car racing. Though he retired from driving in 1992, Petty is now active as a team owner.

No longer just a venue for auto-related sponsors, NASCAR has become a hotbed for blue-chip corporations. Anheuser-Busch's Budweiser brand has been a long-time sponsor.

Patty Moise is one of only a handful of women to have competed in one of NASCAR's top levels.

In the hours before a race, a crewman prepares tires to be used in the event.

Jeff Gordon's "Rainbow Warriors" pit crew will change four tires and dump two cans of gasoline into the car in about 20 seconds.

Pit road during a race is the life center for the teams. Here each team will have virtually everything needed to make minor and major repairs within arm's reach.

With seven Winston Cup championships, Dale Earnhardt is tied with Richard Petty for the most series' titles. Earnhardt has been called the greatest driver ever by many observers of the sport.

During practice sessions leading up to the race, teams will change motors and other parts in an attempt to gain the optimum set up for their drivers.

Terry Labonte's Kellogg's Corn Flakes-backed team swaps motors in an effort to give him just a bit more power.

With movie-star good looks and superb on-track abilities, Jeff Gordon, the 1995 Winston Cup champion, has become the image of the sport in the '90s.

Exide Batteries-sponsored driver Jeff Burton is one of the sport's up and coming stars.

Jeff Green, the 1994 Busch Grand National champion, made the move to Winston Cup racing in 1997.

Interstate Batteries-sponsored driver Bobby Labonte speaks to the fans following his 1996 NAPA 500 win at the Atlanta Motor Speedway.

Rusty Wallace, the 1989 Winston Cup champion, talks strategy with his crew chief Robin Pemberton and fellow crew members.

Dale Earnhardt ponders his performance in practice while his crew makes adjustments to his car.

NASCAR's inspectors check over every car in the hours before each race. The body of each model must fit several specific templates.

After inspection and before the race, teams use generators to supply power to heaters around the oil tank. Warm oil helps cars get up to maximum speed quickly.

Dale Earnhardt's Goodwrench-sponsored crew goes to work.

Driver Ernie Irvan discusses the performance of his car in practice with then crew chief Larry McReynolds. McReynolds now guides Dale Earnhardt's efforts.

Cable television's Cartoon Network uses this vehicle to promote its animated programming such as "The Flintstones." The channel is just one of the dozens of non-automotive sponsors trying to reach consumers through stock car racing.

A race comes to an early end for the Cartoon Network Wacky Racing Team.

NASCAR's mandate for a level playing field produces close racing action at most venues.

ivers will make dozens of laps alone in practice sessions trying to find the ht combination of shocks, springs and tire pressure to produce the fastest eds.

The heart of every Winston Cup racer is a 358 cubic-inch engine capable of producing upwards of 750 horsepower.

Before qualifying, the car's front air ducts are taped over to cut down wind resistance. For race day, the ducts are opened to allow fresh air into the motor and brakes.

Unlike any other sport, NASCAR allows fans into the garages, racing's equivalent to the locker room, in the hours leading up to a race. Here, Rusty Wallace talks with NASCAR flagman Doyle Ford and some fans.

A crew member scrapes debris off a tire to check the surface.

Often, races are won and lost in the pits. In the 60's, pit stops often exceeded 60 seconds. The same work is now done in one-third the time.

Members of Geoff Bodine's QVC-sponsored team make adjustments to the rear end of his Thunderbird during a practice session.

In order to speed up at pit stop time, crews glue the lugnuts onto the wheels before the race begins. Doing so eliminates the need for tire changers to fumble with the bolts during pit stops when time matters most.

One of the most frightening things for a driver to ever see in his rear-view mirror: Dale Earnhardt's black No. 3 Goodwrench Monte Carlo.

Two drivers battle for position at the high-banked Dover Downs
International Speedway, also known as "The Monster Mile."

Television ratings were up 10 percent for races that aired on ABC and CBS in 1996, according to Nielsen Media Research statistics. CBS' coverage of the 1996 Daytona 500 averaged a 9.2 rating (percentage of the 97 million homes with TVs in the country). Overall, the network averaged a 6.1 rating for its Winston Cup telecasts, which represented an increase of 20 percent over 1995 and an increase of 22 percent since 1990.

ABC aired two events in 1996 for an average of a 4.9 rating, representing a year-to-year increase of 11 percent and a 23 percent boost since 1990.

Winston Cup telecasts on ESPN were up 8 percent in 1996 and a whopping 50 percent since 1990. TNN has seen its racing ratings grow 29 percent since its first race in 1990 and TBS is up 44 percent since 1990.

A cumulative total of 148,758,000 people tuned into the 31 Winston Cup telecasts in 1996, according to Nielsen Media Research. Those figures account for the total viewership for each race during the season, meaning a viewer was counted separately for each race he or she watched. However, on average, the races drew an estimated audience of 4,798,645 people.

Recent growth notwithstanding, ratings of stock car telecasts lag behind football, though are higher than both regular season baseball and hockey.

How high they can go also remains to be seen. In 1993 ESPN launched ESPN2 and committed a sizeable portion of its schedule to autoracing coverage. TNN has added to its stable of race and motorsports informational programming. Speedvision has numerous recap and highlight shows. And, of course, the broadcast networks have their lineups of race telecasts. Yet, based on viewer reaction, it appears that there is plenty of room for growth ahead.

"I don't know how much is too much," said Wheeler. "We need to improve the quality. There is a lot of quantity out there. If the ratings continue to increase, I don't know when the quantity of the shows is going to peak out."

From Trackside to Your Home

Though it seems rather easy to put a race of any kind on the air, it's really a rather complicated technical process that takes many more hours and people than what viewers see while sitting in their easy chairs.

To get one five-hour race telecast together, producers, directors, assistants, on-air talent and others will literally work several days.

Typically, work for a Sunday race telecast begins sometime on Thursday when the big rigs hauling mobile broadcasting units pull into the racing facility. At most tracks, the trucks are parked outside of the facility, near the press box. This cordoned off area is referred to by those in the business as the TV compound.

The mobile units provide show producers with virtually every tool necessary to create and control a television program including audio equipment, video tape playback, editing, graphics and the command center, which consists of a panel of small TV screens from which the director will call the shots that eventually turn up on your television set.

As soon as the truck is parked and set up, program staffers, usually free-lancers who have been flown in for the show, will go about laying the cabling needed for audio and video feeds around the track. According to World Sports' Wheeler, at a marquis facility such as Charlotte, the production will require about 100,000 feet or just over 19 miles of cable to be put in place.

It costs about $250,000 to put on a top-notch telecast, though it can be done for less if producers use fewer cameras and people.

"So much work goes into the event before Thursday," Wheeler said. "Then they [the production team] travel from all over the country, assemble in an empty parking lot, and in a day convert it to a full-fledged television studio."

By Thursday evening, the technical aspect of the production is complete. On Friday of race week, producers and on-air talent will conduct interviews and shoot raw footage of the competitors that will later be edited into packages for airing during the race telecast. This is the time when they'll collect head shots for use during pre-race telecasts.

No matter what network is airing the main event, they'll usually also carry the support race held on Saturday. Those races will either be a Busch Series, or an Automobile Racing Club of America event or a NASCAR Craftsman Truck Series race. While not technically taxing on the television crew, it does, however, give them a chance to test all of the camera angles and audio hook ups before the Winston Cup race.

To cover a race at Charlotte, World Sports employs 80 people, uses two helicopters, and deploys about 22 cameras in various positions around the race track, according to Wheeler.

Eight of the cameras will be mounted in fixed positions around the race track. Six or seven cars will be equipped with in-car cameras. One camera is affixed to a helicopter. Three roaming cameras will go along with the pit-road reporters (these provide the shots of crew chiefs during the race). One camera will be placed in a portable infield studio. Two small cameras will be placed on the outside wall near the start-finish line to deliver what announcers refer to as the "speed shot." And another will be devoted to roaming through several areas in the grandstands ranging from the flag stand, to the control booth to random shots of fans in the stands.

While every fan surely wants their favorite driver to carry an in-car camera it's actually the sponsors who decide whether the team gets a camera or not. Depending on the network carrying the race, sponsors will pay anywhere from $10,000 to $20,000 to have their cars equipped with the devices.

"It's very expensive to do," Wheeler said. "It basically covers the cost of production."

Indeed, including in-car cameras in the mix is a mini-production in its own right. The cameras and technology are produced by an outside company. Each car will carry three cameras, placed in NASCAR and team approved positions. Electronic devices in the cars send the video signals to a helicopter which is kept hovering over the race track for the duration of the event. The signal bounces off the helicopter and down to a small antenna usually mounted at the top of the grandstands. The signal then travels by cable to a remote truck that deals with the in-car cameras. From there the signal is fed into the main production truck to be used at the director's discretion.

All of the in-car cameras, of course, are electronically controlled by a producer who has the ability to pan and tilt each unit. Some of the more popular spots are in the rear of the car looking forward, which also gives images looking out of the side windows (referred to as the doggie cam); on the dashboard or passenger side of the car looking at the driver; on the undercarriage aimed at the wheels or axles; and in front or rear bumpers. In early 1997, NASCAR banned roof-mounted cameras after wind-tunnel tests indicated teams with the cameras gained more downforce.

In recent years, the networks have outfitted crew members with helmet cameras to provide viewers with a bird's-eye view of a team member in action. And for a couple of years CBS had a remote-controlled helicopter armed with a small camera to provide aerial views of pit road.

"The primary issue with the in-car camera is that it makes the drive look real easy," said Wheeler. "They don't depict all of the bouncing around these guys go through during the race."

NASCAR has the final say on where in-car cameras can be placed, though before NASCAR rules, the teams have discussed the options with the television producers. It's unlikely that NASCAR would approve a camera position without the team's support. When mounting cameras in cars, teams usually have the same concerns as NASCAR. Will it fall off and injure the driver? And will it expose too much proprietary information to other teams? If the answer is no to both questions, the placement is usually approved.

Teams are also usually concerned about the positioning of the camera's control unit and any weight it may add to the car.

Despite the huge costs involved on the sponsor's part, there is no written guarantee that the car will receive any set amount of coverage during the race telecast. If a car wrecks early, the sponsor is out the cash. If there's a technical breakdown on the part of the network, the sponsor will get another in-car opportunity down the road at no cost.

The cameras that work pit road work in a similar fashion as the in-car set ups. Each pit road camera crew includes a camera operator, a sound specialist, an assistant for the on-air talent, and a pointer. The pointer's job is to aim a large pole towards the roof of the main grandstand. The pole sends a radio signal carrying the footage from the pits to a catcher located high about the track. From there the signal is fed down to the production trailers and into the main control room.

Once the event is underway, overall responsibility for the race is left to the producer who, according to Wheeler, is "the story teller." The producer will be in constant contact with the on-air announcers through tiny ear pieces. For instance, the producer may tell the announcers that in a few seconds they're going to cut to the action on pit road. Then once the video from pit road is available, the on-air personalities will start describing the action. Other times, the producer will signal the talent to be ready to talk about an instant replay that has been cued up. Or, perhaps most important, when it's time to take a commercial break.

Wheeler usually spends a race day putting out fires and trying to make the event coverage run smoothly.

"The biggest challenge," said Wheeler, "is how do you cover a race? How do you decide what stories to tell? Racing is one of the toughest things to do because you have 40 balls on the court at the same time. And because of the size of the venue. Few other sports have that expanse."

Wheeler believes television does a very good job in telling the story of the race. Where TV fails, she said, is delivering "the bodily experience" of racing, which involves the gut-rumbling felt when 43 cars go wide open down the front-stretch and the energy created when tens of thousands of people are crammed into bleachers.

Technically, delivering all of that experience may never be possible. However, there are some things that Wheeler and other producers would try if NASCAR and the teams would only approve.

World Sports would like to include more telemetry to the telecasts, which would provide such information as speed, rpms and other aspects of the car's performance. In addition, Wheeler would like to wire drivers with sensors that would provide viewers with details about the driver's vital signs. Such technology has been incorporated into race telecasts of other series.

"It's a much more loud and bodily event in person than it is on television," Wheeler said. "It's so hard to get that across on television: the sound, the smell, the social experience. There's incredible energy there."

10

SAFETY

Making Sure Everyone Gets Home

Ricky Craven remembers little of the spectacular 1996 wreck that horrified race fans around the country as they watched it unfold on live television.

On April 28, 1996, while running at speeds near 190 mph, Mark Martin and Jeff Gordon collided on lap 130 of the Winston Select at the 2.66-mile Talladega Superspeedway. As often happens in these high-speed wrecks, cars went in all directions attempting to avoid the initial crash. During the melee, Craven's No. 41 Kodiak Chevrolet was struck. It flipped violently, flew over a handful of spinning cars and bounced off a steel retaining fence several feet above the outside wall of the speedway.

In a matter of seconds, the car slammed down onto the apron of the speedway, a fraction of what it was before the crash. Had the retaining fence not been in place, Craven most certainly would have sailed out of the raceway.

Craven, one of the sport's brightest new stars, suffered a minor compression of a vertebra, a bruised lung, multiple bruises on his body, and a black eye.

"I have a hard time remembering the incident," Craven said a few days after the wreck. "I remember Mark [Martin] being sideways and I know I got hit or went over the top of Mark or something. Then I just can't really put it all together."

Though badly banged up and sore, Craven was grateful he wasn't hurt worse.

"I woke up in the hospital and saw the replay on TV," Craven said, "and I thought, 'I feel sorry for that poor driver' and then I realized it was me."

If the same incident occurred just three decades earlier, Craven would not have fared so well. The roll cage, the heart of any stock car, maintained its integrity and saved Craven from more serious injuries. The remainder of the car, however, was scrap.

"We assume some risk when we do this," Craven said. "I knew that when I began this career. I feel the way I do because of the mechanical understanding of what goes into the race cars. I don't think they're designed to come apart, but they certainly absorb a lot of the punishment, and that's what you saw in our incident. The first thing to come off were the tires and then the bumpers, which are built to absorb some of the compression and inertia."

Fact is, Craven suffered the hardest hit of the entire wreck when the car landed on the apron at the end. Without much of the suspension or tires left on the car, there was nothing to break the fall.

Like most drivers who have lived through similar situations, Craven wanted the car to be used as an example of how well NASCAR cars are designed for safety.

"I wouldn't mind the public seeing this car," Craven said.

Craven is not alone. In July 1996, seven-time Winston Cup champion Dale Earnhardt was sent spinning at Talladega and went barrel-rolling down a straightaway. Throughout the ordeal, his car was banged and pushed, including a direct hit to the roof of the driver's compartment. And a couple of years ago, Rusty Wallace flipped numerous times at Daytona, in a wreck that left him with minor injuries. In each of these terrifying incidents, the driver survived because the structure of the vehicle stayed together and protected its passenger.

Increasing the safety of the drivers is a relatively recent concern in the motorsports world. Many of the safety devices in place today — hailed as lifesavers — didn't exist in the '60s. Then, more often than not, the introduction of a new safety function was met with resistance, mostly because of the amount of weight it added to the cars.

Take a look at pictures of the drivers from the '60s or earlier. They wore flimsy helmets and short-sleeved shirts. Safety functions were limited to a crude roll-bar set up, a helmet and a seat belt — which wasn't introduced until 1953. Drivers caught in accidents involving fire were usually badly burned. Death was a more common part of racing.

Both Wallace and Craven, and all the other drivers on the Winston Cup circuit, can thank those drivers who came before — some who lost their lives — for the safety equipment in place today.

Bill Simpson, founder of Simpson Race Products, has spent most of his life working to prevent deaths and serious injuries in motorsports. Up until the '70s, Simpson admits he was fighting an uphill battle.

"It had been that way for a long time," Simpson said. "I don't think it became a factor until the mid-'60s. It has not been overnight, it's been an evolution."

Simpson got his start in the safety business as a 17-year-old creating parachutes to stop high speed dragsters. He later went on to become an Indy Car driver in 1969.

Today, thanks to Simpson and other concerned manufacturers, drivers are safer than ever.

But it has taken literally decades to get there. Because of the relative lack of concern in the early days of the sport, it often took a death or serious injury to spark someone to create or change something to make it safer for drivers. Each wreck became a learning tool for folks like Simpson.

"Now it's a big issue," he said. "It used to be a constant fight to get people to listen. If you go back to those days there were a lot of people killed in motor racing — 30 or 40 a year. It had to stop and it has. Today, there are five fatalities worldwide."

In broad strokes, there are a handful of major components that make up a total safety package of a Winston Cup driver.

Firesuits

Firesuits were first introduced to Winston Cup racing in 1967, four years after drag racers made them part of their standard equipment. The early suits were made from the material used on the parachutes that slowed the fall of space craft, Simpson said.

"The old suits didn't breathe very well," Simpson said.

According to Simpson, firesuits in 1967 protected drivers from fire for about seven seconds. The current suits used by most drivers provide up to 40 seconds of protection from fire.

Before firesuits, some drivers would soak their clothing in a fire retardant chemical. While their clothes were allegedly fire resistant, they were also stiff as a board.

NASCAR's rules only require that drivers wear firesuits. There are no provisions forcing them to wear flame resistant gloves, shoes or face protectors. Rulebook notwithstanding, most drivers do wear gloves and shoes. Some, however, continue to drive without them.

"I get really irritated [when drivers don't wear gloves]," Simpson said. "I shouldn't. I'm not their conscience. I can say something to them, that I don't think it's right, and that if something should happen they're going to have a problem. Young kids look at me like I'm their father."

In 1996 an incident occurred during the season-ending Busch Grand National event at Homestead in Miami, when Mike Laughlin, Jr. slammed into the wall. His car burst into flames as it came to a stop, trapping Laughlin inside. He eventually climbed out, his firesuit still smoldering. The suit worked, protecting his body from burns. However, the only major injuries he suffered were serious burns to his hands. He wasn't wearing gloves.

Helmets

When designing products, Simpson looks for ways of limiting the impact of a crash. With helmets, which represent a large portion of Simpson's product line, the idea is to create one that absorbs the force of a crash.

"In a nasty accident, we want the helmet to fall apart," Simpson said. "We want to dissipate the force of the impact. There's a fine line. When the driver starts getting banged up, the helmet is supposed to start delaminating and cracking."

Helmets are tested by dropping them from a height of 18 feet onto a solid concrete pad covered by steel. A device measures how many G forces the head would absorb in the fall.

"Any force absorbed by the helmet is force not going to the driver's head," Simpson said.

The biggest challenge facing sanctioning bodies and makers of safety products is dealing with sudden deceleration injuries, Simpson said. Sudden deceleration is when the car stops short — as well as the body of the driver — while his internal organs continue moving. Such incidents usually result in death or severe brain damage. Neil Bonnett's 1994 death at Daytona has been attributed to such an occurrence as has Ernie Irvan's injuries suffered in a wreck at Michigan in 1995.

"There's really nothing I can do about it as a helmet designer," Simpson said. "It's something the car builders are working on."

Fuel Cells

Helping reduce the risk of fire in race cars is the fuel cell, a flexible gas tank designed not to burst with the force of a wreck. The first cells, which were rubber bladders, were introduced in the mid-'60s.

"They were a far cry from what they are today," Simpson said. "Today you can shoot at them."

The fuel cells came into play after a series of wrecks that resulted in fires, including a 1964 incident that took the life of Glenn (Fireball) Roberts, who at the time was one of the sport's biggest stars.

NASCAR requires fuel cells to be mounted inside a steel box and then affixed in between safety bars within the rear of the chassis.

Before fuel cells, cars hit in the rear would often burst into flames as bending sheetmetal and frame parts punctured the steel gas tank. Fuel cells in use to today, however, are created to withstand such impact and prevent gasoline from spilling out onto the track or hot parts.

The cell consists of three main parts. A bladder is made of Kelvar, the same material used in bulletproof vests to withstand impact. Synthetic foam inserts reduce the amount of sloshing inside the bladder as gas is used up. And a steel container holds the entire bladder.

Under NASCAR's current rules, fuel cells should be changed five years after their date of manufacture, which is stamped on every cell.

Fires do still happen, though not as frequently as they once did. And should a fire occur, each car has a fire extinguisher system built in that is controlled by the driver. If fire breaks out, he can reach over and activate the system while trying to free himself.

The Roll Cage

The cornerstone of any stock car today is the roll cage. This tangled web of steel tubing creates a protective cocoon around the driver.

Introduced in the '50s, the roll cage, which is an integral part of the chassis, has been consistently improved and built on over the years.

In the '50s, the cage consisted of just a handful of bars made from the equivalent of plumber's tubing. At one point in time, drivers piloted convertibles without tops and only a few roll bars, if any. Yet, cars caved in during serious wrecks, causing serious injuries to the drivers.

The design of the cage has changed over the years because of necessity. Like most areas of racing, the alterations have usually been the result of a tragic accident from which car builders and NASCAR have found that a bar placed in a specific area may have prevented some injury or even death to the driver.

Every accident is a learning tool for car builders and the sanctioning body. The most recent change to the cage was the addition of a bar running down the center of the windshield connected to the top portion of the cage prior to the 1997 season. The bar had been talked about before the 1996 season, however, when Earnhardt wrecked at Talladega in 1996, it became clear there was a need for the bar. During the crash, Earnhardt was hit on the roof, just above his head. The impact crushed the top roll cage downward. While he wasn't injured in that portion of the wreck, all agreed more steel was necessary to keep the roof from caving in on the driver.

Incidents like Earnhardt's crash as well as constant tinkering by car builders leads to improvements in safety functions.

"If we have an idea, or any car builder has an idea, we do it and let NASCAR see it," said Ronnie Hopkins, Jr., president of RHE Inc., a leading car builder based in South Carolina. "Sometimes it comes from crashes, when we can see where things break or could be dangerous to the drivers."

There are several bars and tubes that make up the standard Winston Cup chassis set up. Each has specific functions, whether to bend or break or stay stiff during a crash.

According to Hopkins, the bars making up the central part of the roll cage are made with tubing that is 1 3/4 inches wide with a tubing wall .090 of an inch thick. Those toward the front and rear of the cars that are designed to flex in a crash are made of .065-inch thick wall tubing.

"It's designed so that as it gets closer to the driver it won't bend," Hopkins said.

A complete chassis weighs just 600 lbs, according to Hopkins. His company will make about 115 chassis each year, with roughly 75 percent made for Winston Cup teams.

Seats and Seat Belts

Under NASCAR's rules when the sport started, the cars had to be stock. That included the seats and the seat belts that drivers used during the race.

In the '50s and '60s, cars had large front bench seats. So did stock car drivers. Seat belts didn't come into play until the mid '50s and then they were just simple lap belts similar to those supplied with the street versions.

Drivers didn't much mind those flimsy belts because they provided them with the freedom to duck down in the case of a crash, in which the roof normally caved in.

The downside to the bench seats was that they provided no help in keeping the driver stable against the G forces involved when driving fast in the turns.

The introduction of bucket seats into street cars was the first step toward the seats used today. The buckets offered drivers something a bit more comfortable than the bench seat.

Meanwhile, driver's looked to the aeronautics industry for ways to improve the seat belt system. In the early '60s, pilots started using a shoulder harness to keep them in their seats. Stock car drivers would shop army surplus stores for used harnesses and then install them into their race cars.

Seats and safety belts have now evolved into integral components of a Winston Cup car. Today's aluminum seats are formed to engulf the driver. They provide support for the head, body and legs against the strong forces incurred during a race and in accident situations.

Drivers are strapped into their seats using a five point safety harness. The belts keep the drivers secure in their seats, although allow easy access in emergency situations.

NASCAR requires that all seatbelts be replaced every two years. Simpson would rather have teams change them once a year or more should they come under great stress.

Roof Flaps and Roof Rails

One risk of driving sleek 3,400-lb race cars at high speeds is going airborne during wrecks.

Cars spinning on the superspeedways are subject to a change in air pressure that creates the same sort of lift that makes airplanes fly. Winston Cup cars are subject to this situation in instances when the car is spinning backwards or, most often, at a 45-degree angle to the speedway.

In the early '90s, NASCAR was faced with the growing number of cars flipping over during wrecks at the high-speed ovals such as Talladega and Daytona. Mark Martin, for example, was turned around at Talladega during a race in 1991. The rear of his car sailed into the air — nearly standing upright on its nose — until he collided with another car. There were a rash of similar incidents in which a car turned sideways or all the way around in a crash and flipped over.

NASCAR attempted to cut down on such incidents by installing small strips of metal along the outside of the roof and down the rear window. The theory was that the rails would break the airflow and therefore help keep the cars on the ground.

Those bars led, in part, to the creation of the roof-flaps that are standard in all Winston Cup cars today.

Jack Roush, owner of the Winston Cup cars driven by Mark Martin, Ted Musgrave and Jeff Burton, a leading innovator of racing technology, designed the roof flaps after watching too many terrible crashes.

The design is simple: Two flaps roughly 6" by 14" are placed at slightly different angles and mounted flush with the rear portion of the roof. The flaps are attached by hinges and cables. Once a car goes spinning, the change in air pressure lifts the flaps open and cuts the flow of air over the roof which, in the past, would have created the lifting action.

Since the flaps have been introduced, the number of cars flipping over for aerodynamic reasons has been reduced significantly, although it does still happen.

Window Nets

Drivers can thank Richard Petty for window nets.

While racing at Darlington in 1970, Petty was involved in a horrifying wreck during which his car slammed into the inside retaining wall and then went tumbling down the track's straightaway.

Most troubling, however, are the images of Petty's arms and shoulder — which was broken — dangling from the car as it landed upside down on the speedway.

As is the case with most of NASCAR's safety innovations, officials and drivers used the crash as a way to better protect themselves. Soon after, early forms of the window net were introduced as a way to keep the driver's arms — or any other part — from hanging out of the car, and to protect drivers from anything that may sail into the car.

Window nets took on an added dimension in the early '90s following wrecks in which the roofs of the cars were torn off allowing the drivers' hands to dangle out of the car. Some drivers started installing a version of the window net on the top portion of the roll cage commonly referred to as the halo.

Learning from Wrecks

Following every serious accident, guys like Simpson and Hopkins turn into racing's equivalent of coroners. Each wreck provides a victim — the car — from which they'll be able to determine how well the safety system held up. Those autopsies often lead to new products or design changes that may eventually spare another driver from injury or death.

"Usually when there's been a wreck I go to the shop and ask for permission to inspect the stuff," Simpson said. "I look at the seat belt, I look at the seat to see what happened. . . . You look at the aftermath to see if there is something you can fix."

According to Simpson, he'd never seen a set of seat belts so deformed as he did when he checked out Craven's car following the Talladega wreck. "The hardware was stretched, the webbing took a helluva impact."

In the case of Craven's seatbelts, Simpson said he suggests drivers change their belts more frequently. A set of seat belts goes for about $100.

"When you see a wreck, and when the car gets hit in an awkward position," said Hopkins, "you think the driver could be hit. The statistics of NASCAR and the drivers getting hurt is real good. I know when everybody watches a wreck most of the time we assume they'll be okay."

People involved with overseeing safety issues in NASCAR racing are quick to point out that there is no single aspect of the package more important than the other. It's the combination of all of those factors that make the series as safe as it is today.

"If you were to go back to the '60s and had an accident like Rusty [Wallace] had at Daytona or Talladega," Simpson said, "Rusty wouldn't be with us anymore."

TECHNOLOGY TRANSFER

Racing for a Reason

You've seen the commercials and the newspaper advertisements. The auto makers and other companies supplying parts to the motorsports field want you to think that somehow their 500-mile races on Sunday will in some way make your ride to work better.

Considering the vast differences between the street versions and those running on the Winston Cup Series, it's hard to believe there could be anything they could do in race conditions that would help.

In reality, the idea of racing helping consumer products isn't that far fetched. In fact, there are a lot of ways that motorsports companies are contributing improvements in street-car technology.

Take Ford for example. The company's motorsports advertisements all carry the tag line: "We Race. You Win." According to John Valentine, chief engineer of Motorsport Technology for the company, the tag line is not an exaggeration.

Ford is not alone in using racing to advance car technology. Indeed, each of the manufacturers has a specific division set up to push motorsports and promote the company to consumers. Ford is, however, a good example of how the process works.

"Basically, we're using racing as a test bed," Valentine said. "We're trying to put pieces into race cars for evaluation and quick assessment. Of course, we're always interested in winning. We're extremely interested in that. But even if we don't win, the point is we're getting our money's worth out of our racing involvement."

While Ford does extensive research in Winston Cup, it's just as heavily involved in experimentation in Indy car, Trans Am and Formula One racing. Where the company decides to test a product depends on the the race series and the application.

For instance, if they were to test a new type of brake pad, it's likely the company would focus on the Trans Am series which is run on demanding road courses that would better replicate what a passenger vehicle would experience.

Conversely, both the Indy car and Formula One series use turbo charged engines, where technology could be transferred back to passenger vehicles.

"We try to match what we're trying to study with a race series," Valentine said. "We focus on the three Ps — people, product and process."

To that end, Ford places company trained engineers on teams within each race series. In NASCAR, there is a Ford-paid staffer on Robert Yates' Winston Cup team. The engineers live and work with the teams for a period of two years. During that time they'll work on specific projects, such as engine design or computer analysis. Once the two-year program is over, the engineers return to Ford to work on a production line.

"When training engineers it's a really good thing to put them in a racing situation for awhile," Valentine said. "It gives them a great overall view of what's going on in relation to racing. We want them to come from general mainstream engineering and we want them to go back to mainstream engineering."

In fact, after two years in the program, most of the engineers are ready to come back to a regular job. There are surely glamorous aspects to the sport, but it's very demanding in terms of hours and workload. "I think after 30 weekends of NASCAR traveling, Darlington starts to look an awful lot like Talladega," Valentine joked.

Before the engineer goes to work for a team, Ford and the team owner usually work out an agreement on how any new technology developed under the partnership will be implemented. Usually, if something revolutionary sprouts from the relationship the team will generally have exclusive use of the item for a set period of time, say six races.

The engineer-in-residence program goes both ways, too. In addition to Ford placing staffers on race teams, teams also send their engineers to Detroit to work within Ford's technology center. "They're generally working on race-related stuff," Valentine said. "Generally, using our test facilities to do analysis for the team. While the teams are physically here, the data becomes the property of the Ford Motor Company."

So what is Ford actually working on that might make it into passenger car use?

During the 1996 and 1997 seasons, Ford has been using the Winston Cup Series to test advanced radiator cores, which could some day make their way into passenger car applications. The company has also developed a light-weight starter motor, now being used on the Busch Grand National Series. And there are engine parts such as valve lifters being developed for racing that could end up in high-performance street cars.

Aside from training people, Ford uses racing to check its computer modeling of how cars react in racing conditions. It also uses the sport to develop new ways of producing parts for race cars and for passenger vehicles. For example, Ford's Cosworth racing engine unit developed a process to cast engine blocks, which is likely to be used for the next generation of Ford consumer motors.

"It's not only parts," Valentine said, "it's process as well."

And research isn't limited to making cars go faster, either. Ford has installed sensors on cars in Indy car and Formula One to collect data on the forces on a car and the driver in crashes. The data will help company designers better understand the limits of human tolerance, much the way crash dummies are used in passenger car tests.

"It's almost accident investigation, but probably more in-depth," Valentine explained. "It gives us an overall analysis of what happened in the wreck."

That information, he said, would go toward building stronger race cars and ultimately better passenger cars.

"Henry Ford began using motorsports when he first founded the company to establish a name and technology leadership," Valentine said. "It's still there today."

Virtually every automotive company involved with racing is using the sport to some extent as a test bed. Motor oil manufacturers, such as Pennzoil and Valvoline, use it to test the durability of their products, which are also sold to consumers. And many of the autoparts makers who are also contingency sponsors such as Stant, Autometer, Edlebrock and Jesel make products for high-end consumer applications.

Goodyear, which supplies all of the tires used on the Winston Cup circuit, develops race-related technology that transfers to its passenger car lines. Already, consumers have benefited from Goodyear's racing rain treads created for the Formula One and Indy car series, which have turned up on the company's Eagle passenger car tires. Other passenger tire features created through racing include low-profile sidewalls, wide treads and wraparound tread compounds.

"One of the things we're doing as a racing division, is we have begun to develop and submit tires for original equipment supercars, mainly Ferraris," said Stu Grant, general manager, racing worldwide for Goodyear. "The Ferrari you see on the streets are very race-like."

Usually, when an auto manufacturer is looking for a tire for a new street car, they'll go though the passenger car tire division of Goodyear. However, when the super-fast Ferraris needed new treads, the program was handed over to the racing division.

"This was a major change in terms of development flow and cooperation," Grant said.

Of course, as the sole tire supplier to Winston Cup, Goodyear also gets a sizeable promotional bump week in and week out. Fact is, the Goodyear tires used on race cars and those used on top-level passenger cars are both called Eagles, giving the consumer a basic impression that they're running tires that are somehow connected to Dale Earnhardt's.

Goodyear, like Ford, uses racing as a way to train engineers. While they may not have competition on the race track, the company does face numerous competitors on the street. And because racing is a fast-paced environment, it serves as a great place to train engineers to step up their response to needs on the consumer side.

Drivers of Chrysler's high-end line of automobiles have Bill Simpson, founder of Simpson Race Products, to thank for the seat belts in their cars. They've been produced using the same technology that Simpson has used for decades to make race cars safer for drivers.

Ultimately, companies use racing because there is no tougher environment to test a product than in actual race conditions. If a product can withstand race situations, street use should prove no problem. Success on the track also generates favorable impressions with consumers.

"I think there's a parallel between racing and the actual production side that is very important and people tend to forget about," Valentine said. "In building production vehicles there are government regulations and standards that must be met. In all of racing there are also standards and rules that must be met. There are cost considerations in building production cars. And there are definitely cost considerations in racing. There's a due date in production cars and that also holds true in racing. You've got to be there when the season opens and you've got to be there every race day. "

THE TRACKS

Stock Car Racing's Sports Palaces

Atlanta Motor Speedway

P.O. Box 500
Hwys 19 & 41
Hampton, GA 30228

Length: 1.54 miles
Degree of banking in corners: 24
Degree of banking in straights: 5

The Atlanta Motor Speedway was built in 1960 and has since been turned into a fixture on the NASCAR circuit. The first Winston Cup race, then called Grand National, was held in July 1960.

AMS was overhauled following the March 1997 running of the Primestar 500. The track, a true-oval, was converted into a quad-oval similar to its sister tracks, the Charlotte Motor Speedway and Texas Motor Speedway. The frontstretch became the back and dog-leg turns were added to the new frontstretch.

The track is owned by Speedway Motorsports, which also counts among its holdings such tracks as the Charlotte, Texas, Bristol International Speedway and Sears Point.

Overlooking the track is 1500 Tara Place, a nine-story building containing 46 condominium suites, a feature that has become a trademark for Speedway Motorsports properties.

In addition to the 1.54-mile oval, AMS is home to a 2.5-mile road course.

The track is located 30 miles south of downtown Atlanta on US Highways 19-41, in Hampton, Georgia.

Ticket information: P.O. Box 500, Hampton, GA 30228. Phone: (770) 946-4211. Nearest airport: Hartsfield International Airport. Local information: The Atlanta Chamber of Commerce, (404) 880-9000.

Bristol Motor Speedway

P.O. Box 3966
Hwy 11 East & Volunteer Pkwy
Bristol, TN 37625

Length: .533 miles
Degree of banking in corners: 36
Degree of banking on straights: 16
Length of frontstretch: 650 ft.
Length of backstretch: 650 ft.

Located in the hills of Northern Tennessee, Bristol lays claim to being the fastest half-mile track on the Winston Cup circuit. It only takes a glance of the track's high banks — the steepest in the series — to see why the action is so fast.

The track opened in 1961 and held its first race in July of that year. The track was redesigned in 1969 to its current configuration. It has been a fan favorite ever since. The front and back of the starting field at Bristol are usually separated by mere hundredths of a second. The closeness of the cars and the tight track usually make for multiple cautions during each event.

Speedway Motorsports acquired the track in 1996 and has rapidly increased capacity at the facility. In 1997, seating at the speedway was 130,000, up from 30,000 when the track opened.

There's not a bad seat in the house. As a result, tickets to Bristol are usually hard to come by.

Ticket information: P.O. Box 3966, Bristol, TN 37325. Phone: (423) 764-1161. Nearest airport: TriCities Airport. Local information: Bristol Chamber of Commerce, (423) 989-4850.

California Speedway
9300 Cherry Ave
Fontana, CA 92335

Length: 2 miles
Degree of banking in corners: 14
Degree of banking in frontstretch: 11
Degree of banking in backstretch: 3
Length of frontstretch: 3,600 ft.
Length of backstretch: 2,242 ft.

California is a newly created facility owned by the Penske Corp. The track is a tri-oval that will initially host one Winston Cup and one Indy car event annually.

The track is on a 512-acre plot known as the historic Kaiser Steel Mill site. At launch, the track's first events are scheduled for 1997 before a crowd of 80,000. Capacity will be increased to eventually accommodate 118,000 fans.

California Speedway is located 40 miles east of Los Angeles. For tickets: (800) 944-7223. Nearest airport: Los Angeles International. For local information: Fontana Chamber of Commerce, (909) 822-4433.

Charlotte Motor Speedway

P.O. Box 600
Hwy 29 North
Concord, NC 28026

Length: 1.5 miles
Degree of banking in corners: 24
Degree of banking in straights: 5
Length of frontstretch: 1,952.8 ft.
Length of backstretch: 1,360 ft.

The Charlotte Motor Speedway has been appropriately dubbed "The Mecca of Motorsports."

With a seating capacity of over 135,000 and growing, the track is the largest sporting venue in the Southeast. And since opening in 1960, it has become the premiere showcase for NASCAR racing in the U.S.

For decades, CMS has served as the hub of the stock car racing industry. About 80 percent of all Winston Cup teams are located within 70 miles of the speedway; many are just a short drive from the speedway itself.

Like its sister track Atlanta, CMS boasts 52 condominiums, as well as executive suites and other fan amenities.

The track is located on US Highway 29, 12 miles north of Charlotte, in Concord. Tickets: P.O. Box 600, Concord, N.C. 28026-0600. Phone: (704) 455-3200. Nearest airport: Charlotte/ Douglas International Airport. Local information: Charlotte Chamber of Commerce, (704) 378-1300.

Darlington Raceway

P.O. Box 500
1301 Harry Byrd Hwy
Darlington, SC 29532-0500

Length: 1.366 miles
Degree of banking in corners (1-2): 25

Degree of banking in corners (3-4): 23
Degree of banking in straights: 2
Length of frontstretch: 1,228 ft.
Length of backstretch: 1,228 ft.

Darlington held its first race in 1950 and officially launched the superspeedway era of NASCAR racing.

Over the years, the track has earned the nickname, "Too Tough To Tame." It is considered one of the toughest tracks on the circuit.

Darlington's egg-shaped surface has two distinctly different turns making it nearly impossible for a team to get the car set up perfectly for both ends of the track. A car that's set up well for one end, won't be right in the other.

For the 1997 season, Darlington underwent a make over. The front stretch became the back and the back the front. The old set up had been there since the first race on September 4, 1950.

The track is located on Highway 151-34, two miles west of Darlington, SC. For tickets: P.O. Box 500, Darlington, SC 29532-0500. Phone: (803) 395-8499. Nearest Airport: Florence City County Airport. Local information: Darlington County Chamber of Commerce, (803) 393-2641.

Daytona International Speedway
P.O. Box 2801 (32120-2801)
1801 West International Speedway Blvd
Daytona Beach, FL 32114-1243

Length: 2.5 miles
Degree of banking in corners: 31
Degree of banking in straights: 6 (18 degrees through tri-oval)
Length of frontstretch: 2,400 ft. in short chutes into tri-oval
Length of backstretch: 3,600 ft.

Daytona International Speedway is often referred to as "The World Center of Racing."

It is the site of the annual Daytona 500, stock car racing's equivalent to football's Super Bowl. It also plays home to the mid-season Pepsi 400, always held on the first Saturday of July.

The track opened in February 1959 and staged its first Winston Cup race that month.

There are permanent seats at Daytona capable of holding nearly 110,000 and another 60,000 fill the infield for the season-opening Daytona 500.

Speeds at Daytona reach 200 mph when cars are running together nose-to-tail in a draft and over 180 mph in the turns. The track record, set by Bill Elliott in 1987 before NASCAR mandated restrictor plates on engines was 210.354 mph.

NASCAR's headquarters and those of the International Speedway Corporation, a subsidiary of NASCAR and the owner of Daytona, are located at the speedway.

The grounds of the facility include a 44-acre lake, which was created when dirt was excavated to create the speedway's 31-degree high-banked turns.

The track is located just east of I-95 on U.S. 92. For tickets: P.O. Box 2801, Daytona Beach, FL 32120. Phone (954) 253-7223. Nearest airport: Daytona Beach International Airport. Local information: Daytona Beach Chamber of Commerce, (904) 255-7311.

Dover Downs International Speedway

P.O. Box 843 (19903)
1131 North Dupont Hwy
Dover, Del. 19901

Length: 1 mile
Degree of banking in corners: 24
Degree of banking in straights: 9
Length of frontstretch: 1,076 ft.
Length of backstretch: 1,076 ft.

Dover Downs International Speedway was built in the late 1960s and held its first Winston Cup event in 1969. In 1971, it expanded to two Winston Cup races annually.

The track goes by the moniker "The Monster Mile," and the handle is no exaggeration. Its high banks and concrete surface make for fast, exciting races, which are great for fans, though grueling on the drivers.

Dover is tough on tires and even tougher on cars. It's not unusual to have a dozen cautions in a Dover event and many more banged up race cars.

Dover's two annual Winston Cup races are the largest sporting events in the state of Delaware. And with future expansion plans that will increase seating to 170,000, the track will certainly maintain its place as the biggest event in the state for a long time to come.

"The Monster Mile" is located on U.S. Route 13, just north of Dover. For tickets: P.O. Box 843, Dover, DE 19903. Phone: (800) 441-7223. Nearest airport: Philadelphia International Airport. For local information: Central Delaware Chamber of Commerce, (302) 734-7513.

Indianapolis Motor Speedway
4790 W. 16th St.
Indianapolis, Ind. 46222

Length: 2.5 miles
Degree of banking in corners: 9
Length of frontstretch: 5/8-mile
Length of backstretch: 5/8-mile
Length of turns: 1/4-mile
Length of short chutes: 1/8-mile

Next to Daytona, there is perhaps no other racing facility as well known as the Indianapolis Motor Speedway. The 2.5-mile oval opened in 1909 as an automotive testing facility.

Over time, early races ruined the tar surface forcing speedway owners to take drastic measures. The facility was then covered with 3.2 million bricks. It has been known as "The Brickyard" ever since.

All but a narrow strip of the original bricks have been covered over with the asphalt surface that remains today. Its 9-degree banking is the flattest of any track on the Winston Cup series.

Indianapolis has been the home of the Indy 500 since 1911. In 1994, NASCAR held its first sanctioned event at the facility called The Brickyard 400. The crowd at Indianapolis for the NASCAR races has been in excess of 300,000, which is the largest ever for a stock car event.

For tickets: P.O. Box 24910, Speedway, IN 46224. Phone: (317) 481-8500. Nearest airport: Indianapolis International Airport. Local information: Indianapolis Chamber of Commerce, (317) 464-2200.

Martinsville Speedway

P.O. Box 3311 (24115-3311)
U.S. 200 South Business
Martinsville, Va. 24112

Length: .526 miles
Degree of banking in corners: 12
Degree of banking in straights: 0
Length of frontstretch: 800 ft.
Length of backstretch: 800 ft.

Martinsville Speedway is the oldest facility on the NASCAR circuit. The half-mile oval was built in 1947 and held its first race that same year.

Martinsville staged its first NASCAR event in 1949 on a dirt surface. In 1955, the track was paved with asphalt.

Today, the track has asphalt straights and cement in the key portions of the turns. With 12-degree banking, Martinsville is the second-flattest on the circuit.

Because of its tight confines, Martinsville is home to some of the closest, fender-rubbing, tire-banging racing in the sport.

The track is located on U.S. 220, just south of Martinsville, VA. For tickets: P.O. Box 3311, Martinsville, VA 24115. Phone: (540) 956-3151. Nearest airport: Piedmont Triad International Airport. For local information: Martinsville/Henry County Chamber of Commerce, (540) 632-6401.

Michigan Speedway
12626 U.S. Highway 12
Brooklyn, Mich. 49230-9068

Length: 2 miles
Degree of banking in corners: 18
Degree of banking in straights: 12 (front), 5 (back)
Length of frontstretch: 3,600 ft.
Length of backstretch: 2,242 ft.

Michigan International Speedway has been part of the Winston Cup series for nearly 30 years.

Its wide racing surface and high banking make it among the fastest on the Winston Cup series. Qualifying speeds are in the 180 mph range, with straightaway speeds tickling the mid-190s.

Two annual Winston Cup events are held at the speedway, which also hosts Indy car events during the year as well.

Michigan opened in 1968 and held its first NASCAR race in 1969.

The track is owned by the Penske Motorsports, which is headed by racing legend Roger Penske. Penske bought the facility in 1973.

Michigan International Speedway is located on U.S. 12, one mile west of M-50 in Brooklyn, MI. For tickets: 12626 U.S. 12, Brooklyn, MI 49230. Phone: (800) 354-1010. Nearest airport: Detroit Metro. For local information: Brooklyn-Irish Hills Chamber of Commerce (517) 592-8907.

New Hampshire International Speedway
P.O. Box 7888
Hwy 106 North
Loudon, N.H. 03301

Length: 1.058 miles
Degree of banking in corners: 12
Length of frontstretch: 1,500 ft.
Length of backstretch: 1,500 ft.

Before Texas and California came onto the circuit, New Hampshire International Speedway had the distinction of being the baby of the NASCAR family.

The track was built in 1990 and began hosting Winston Cup events in 1993. New Hampshire can also lay claim to being the northern-most stop for the series on the East Coast.

For a sport that has been saddled with the incorrect label of being strictly southern, New Hampshire is able to attract more than 80,000 people for its annual Winston Cup events. In 1997, New Hampshire expanded its schedule to two races, with one in July and the other in September. Indeed, nearly 50,000 people will turn out for qualifying and support races the day before the Winston Cup race.

The track is located on Route 106, nine miles north of I-393 in Loudon, NH. For tickets: P.O. Box 7888, Loudon, NH 03301. Phone: (603) 783-4931. Nearest airport: Manchester Airport. For local information: Concord Chamber of Commerce, (603) 224-2508.

North Carolina Motor Speedway
P.O. Box 500
U.S. Hwy 1 North
Rockingham, N.C. 28360

Length: 1017 miles
Degree of banking in corners: (Turns 1-2) 22, (Turns 3-4) 25
Degree of banking in straights: 9
Length of frontstretch: 1,005 ft.
Length of backstretch: 1,030 ft.

The North Carolina Motor Speedway is known to fans and drivers as "The Rock."

Like Darlington, the facility has two different types of turns, making it hard on teams to get a car that handles well on each part of the track.

The force of the cars coming out of turn two tends to push them up near the outside retaining wall, which is the tightest area of the race track. Exiting turn four, the track is wider making it easier for the drivers to stand on the gas.

The North Carolina Motor Speedway is home to the first and last races of each season in the Carolinas.

The track was built in 1965 and held its first Winston Cup race in October of that year.

The Rock is located on U.S. Highway 1, 10 miles north of Rockingham N.C. For tickets: P.O. Box 500, Rockingham, N.C. Phone: (910) 582-2861. Nearest airport: Charlotte/Douglas Airport. For local information: Richmond County Chamber of Commerce, (800) 858-1688.

Phoenix International Raceway
7602 S. 115th Ave.
Avondale, AZ. 85323

Length: 1 mile
Degree of banking in corners: (Turns 1-2) 11, (Turns 3-4) 9
Degree of banking in straights: 0
Length of frontstretch: 1,179 ft.
Length of backstretch: 1,551 ft.

Phoenix has been around since 1964, however it didn't start hosting Winston Cup events until 1988.

The track is nestled between mountains in Phoenix and is known for the huge crowds of people who sit on the dirt hill overlooking the track. That hill, however, is also home to hundreds of rattlesnakes, which are pulled out days before the race by locals. Attendance for Winston Cup races at Phoenix is now more than 100,000 people annually.

Phoenix International Raceway is located six miles off I-10 in Phoenix. For tickets: P.O. Box 13088, Phoenix, AZ 85002. Phone: (800) 638-4253. Nearest airport: Phoenix Sky Harbor. For local information: Arizona Office of Tourism, (602) 542-8687.

Pocono Raceway
P.O. Box 500
Long Pond Road
Long Pond, PA 18334

Length: 2.5 miles
Degree of banking in corners: (Turn 1) 14, (Turn 2) 8, (Turn 3) 6
Length of frontstretch: 3,740 ft.
Length of Long Pond straight: 3,055 ft.
Length of north straight: 1,780 ft.

Nestled in the tourist region of the Pocono Mountains, Pocono Raceway is one of the most competitive tracks on the circuit.

Its three-turn design and long front stretch — which is longer than the entire length of Martinsville — provides drivers with a host of racing hurdles to leap in order to win the race. The wide front stretch often gives fans a bird's eye view of four and five abreast racing.

Pocono's layout forces drivers to shift during the race, which is rare for any track. And in parts the cars will reach speeds near 200 mph.

Pocono was built in 1969, although the tri-oval shape of today wasn't introduced until 1971. It held its first Winston Cup race in 1974.

The track is located three miles south of exit 43 on I-80, on Route 115. For tickets: P.O. Box 500, Long Pond, PA 18334. Phone: (717) 646-2300. Nearest airport: Wilkes Barre Airport. For local information: Pocono Mountains Chamber of Commerce, (717) 421-4433.

Richmond International Raceway

P.O. Box 9257 (23227)
602 East Laburnum Ave
Richmond, Va. 23222

Length: .750 mile
Degree of banking in corners: 14
Degree of banking in straights: front, 8; rear, 2
Length of backstretch: 860 ft.

Richmond International Raceway has been part of NASCAR racing since 1953.

The track started out as a half-mile facility in 1947 and held its first Winston Cup race in April 1953. However, in 1988, it was totally revamped and expanded to its current three-quarter mile format. Today, it stages two Winston Cup races, one held under the lights.

Richmond's grandstand seating can accommodate nearly 85,000 fans.

The track is located at the intersection of I-64 and I-95 on the Virginia State Fairgrounds. For tickets: P.O. Box 9257, Richmond, VA 23227. Phone: (804) 345-7223. Nearest airport: Richmond International Airport. For local information: Richmond Convention and Visitor's Center, (800) 365-7272.

Sears Point Raceway
Highways 37 & 121
Sonoma, Ca. 95476

Length: 2.52 miles
Road Course: 12 turns total, 7 right, 5 left.

Sears Point filled a gap in the Winston Cup circuit for a California-based road course, which was left open when Riverside closed in the late '80s.

The track is in Northern California and sits among some of the finest wineries in the world.

It's one of only two road courses in the series. Like the other, Watkins Glen, Sears Point places a premium on driving skills and durability of the cars. Inexperienced drivers will often attend a road course driving school before attempting to handle the 12-turn course.

Sears Point was constructed in 1968 and held its first Winston Cup race in 1989. In 1996, it was purchased by Speedway Motorsports.

For tickets: Hwys 37, & 121, Sonoma, CA 95476. Phone: (800) 870-7223. Nearest major airport: San Francisco International Airport. For local information: Sonoma Valley Visitor's Bureau, (707) 996-1090.

Talladega Superspeedway
P.O. Box 777
3366 Speedway Blvd
Talladega, Ala. 35161

Length: 2.66 miles
Degree of banking in corners: 33
Degree of banking in straights: front, 18; rear, 2
Length of frontstretch: 4,300 ft.
Length of backstretch: 4,000 ft.

Talladega opened in 1969 and is the fastest track on the circuit.

Restrictor plate racing has slowed speeds dramatically in recent years. However, in 1987, Bill Elliott qualified there at a speed of 212.809 mph.

The addition of power choking restrictor plates has resulted in multi-car packs running on the track and spectacular wrecks.

The 2.66 mile track is the biggest tri-oval on the circuit. It was built at a cost of $4 million and was originally called the Alabama International Motorspeedway.

In 1997, the track underwent extensive upgrading, including the creation of additional skyboxes, and fan amenities.

The track is located 40 miles east of Birmingham on Speedway Boulevard, just off I-20. For tickets: P.O. Box 777, Talladega, AL 35161. Phone: (205) 362-9064 Nearest airport: Birmingham

Municipal Airport. For local information: Greater Talladega Chamber of Commerce, (205) 362-9075.

Texas Motor Speedway
P.O. Box 500
Fort Worth, TX 76101-2500

Length: 1.5 miles
Degree of banking in corners: 24
Degree of banking in straights: 8
Length of frontstretch: 1,952.8 ft.
Length of backstretch: 1,360 ft.

For years NASCAR insiders have discussed expansion of the sport's top level of racing into the Dallas-Ft. Worth marketplace. In 1997, they got their wish with the Texas Motor Speedway, a 1.5-mile oval that draws the best aspects of its sister tracks Atlanta and Charlotte.

The track has 194 skyboxes, served by 21 elevators. Total capacity of the premiere racing venue is nearly 151,000 people, with 120,000 of them sitting in a two-thirds of a mile stretch of grandstand along the front part of the track.

The Texas Motor Speedway is located at the junction of I-35 and Highway 114. For tickets: P.O. Box 500, Fort Worth, TX, 76101-2500. Phone: (817) 215-8500. Nearest airport: Dallas/Fort Worth Airport. For local information: Fort Worth Chamber of Commerce, (817) 336-2491.

Watkins Glen International
P.O. Box 500
500 County Route 16
Watkins Glen, N.Y. 14891

Length: 2.45 miles
Road Course: 11 turns.
Frontstretch: 2,150 feet
Backstretch: 2,600 feet

NASCAR racing has been involved with the upstate New York road course since 1957. Watkins Glen became a staple of the Winston Cup circuit in 1986.

Like Sears Point, Watkins Glen tests the mettle of even the best Winston Cup teams. Driving a road course is more than just having ton of horsepower under the hood. Drivers need to master braking, shifting and acceleration to master Watkins Glen.

Among the track's 11 corners are seven right-hand turns. Attendance is usually more than 130,000 people.

The track is located on Route 14, 15 miles north of Elmira, NY. For tickets: Box 500-T, Watkins Glen, NY 14891. Phone: (607) 535-2481. Nearest airport: Elmira-Corning Airport. For local information: Ithaca Schuyler County Chamber of Commerce, (607) 535-4300.

13

TRAVEL

Getting Around
the NASCAR Circuit

Getting tickets to a big-league stock car race is only half of the battle. The other half, finding a place to stay within the vicinity of the racing venue, can at times be a nerve-wracking experience.

The good news is that with a little bit of planning you can minimize the hassle of getting to a race and increase your enjoyment.

Various surveys indicate that the typical race attendee spends about $400 between tickets, lodging and food during a race weekend. Outside the cost of the ticket, lodging puts the biggest pinch on a NASCAR fan's budget.

But, depending on your ultimate goals and standards of living — loosely translated: how fancy do you need your accommodations — there are ways to cut costs and still have a good, comfortable trip.

You should know straight up that the teams, the sponsors, the manufacturers and virtually everyone else within the traveling NASCAR circus has booked their rooms far in advance. For most of those insiders, the hotel booking process started before the previous season was over. As such, most of the major hotels near the raceway will be full before tickets to the following season's event go on sale to the public. These teams also reserve rooms in bulk, giving them some leeway for the unexpected guest who absolutely, positively, has to be at the race.

After the teams have taken their share, the rest of the available rooms tend to move fast because these are the hotels the tracks recommend to anyone calling for information.

That said, if your goal is to be able to tell your friends that you stayed in the same hotel as the Winston Cup champion and his team, plan on digging deep into your pockets for that benefit. The hotels closest to the track are going to be the most expensive. Like everything else in life, room availability around a race weekend falls under the common business theory of supply and demand. And in the case of Winston Cup racing, the demand far exceeds the supply. It's not unusual to see a hotel triple its normal room rate for a race weekend. Worse yet, they'll often demand folks stay for a minimum number of nights, which also works to push the overall cost of attending an event though the roof.

If you have any inkling that a pair of race tickets may be in your future, pick up the phone and start scouting out hotel options. Hotels hate it, but for now reservations are free. Make the reservation as soon as the notion of going to a race hits you. If the tickets fall through, you can always cancel without penalty as long as you advise the place 48 hours before your scheduled arrival.

There are several ways to find hotels. Begin by calling the track. Often, they'll be able to send a list of nearby establishments. Use this as a starting point. These hotels are likely to be booked by the folks putting on the show. Yet, if told the inn is full, ask for suggestions of nearby facilities that may have rooms available. Hotel managers know what their competition is up to and are apt to know if rooms are available elsewhere.

A call to the local chamber of commerce can also produce a list of hotels. However, don't look to the chamber of commerce to suggest one hotel over the other, or to even provide information on the bad ones. Businesses shell out good money to be part of the local chamber, and the last thing the chamber will do is bad-mouth a member. Also try calling the major hotel chains' toll-free reservation lines. They're an excellent starting point. Each of the chains is equipped with a computer system that will give the customer service operator a first choice and a list of alternate sites for the event. They'll also be able to give estimated distances from the tracks or any other location.

However, if you're calling close to race day, don't fret if the operator says all rooms are booked. If that happens, ask for the hotel's direct telephone number. For race weekends, hotels tend to handle the reservations locally and hold back most of their rooms from the computerized booking computers used by operators on the toll-free lines. If all rooms are booked, you've simply wasted the cost of a long distance call. There again, the hotel manager, who is working in the local market, may be able to suggest a suitable alternative to fit your needs.

If staying at a hotel with the race teams isn't a priority, there are ways to save money, though they'll require a little leg work and perhaps a bit more driving on race day.

First grab a map of the area surrounding the race track. Then start working out from the track. Usually 40–50 miles away is a good place to start. Hotels between 40 and 50 miles away from the track are usually unaffected by the "special event" pricing, meaning they'll be less expensive, and most important, available.

These cheaper rooms also have other benefits. By staying a little farther away you'll skip the long lines and crowds that turn up at restaurants and other attractions near race venues.

Another way to save some money is to join the frequent customer programs offered by most of the big hotel chains. While some programs are limited to small businesses or organizations, others are for regular frequent travelers. There's no cost to sign up for the discount programs and can usually be done by calling the toll-free reservation numbers. These programs regularly send members money-saving coupons good for discounted room rates. And while the hotels close to the track working under the "special event" pricing won't honor the coupons on race weekends, those at the 50-mile radius point usually will.

Moreover, many chains such as Red Roof and Comfort Inns provide an automatic 10 percent discount if the reservation is made from another hotel in the chain. For instance, if there is a Red Roof Inn nearby, go there, pick up the reservation phone in the lobby and make your race-weekend reservations.

Raceday Tips

The bottom line when attending any Winston Cup or stock car racing event is to have fun. There is nothing like the rumble made by 40 Winston Cup stock cars circling the track, or when two cars come to the line neck and neck for the checkered flag.

Making the best of a race day or race weekend takes just a bit of preparation. Here are a few proven tips:

- Get to the track early. Even the best facilities have traffic problems on race day. And who wouldn't with 100,000 people coming to an event? Rest assured, traffic will back up for hours before a race. There is no worse feeling than knowing the race has started before you've made your way into the parking lot. At most tracks there is plenty to do in the hours before the green flag falls. You can browse the many souvenir trailers parked at the track. Many manufacturers and sponsors set up displays and hand out free samples of their products. And at some events the track will have a band or some other form of entertainment available for early birds.
- Wear comfortable shoes. No matter when you get to the track, you'll put a lot of miles on your feet before the day is done.
- Dress in layers. Often it's cool when you get to the track, though as the day goes on the temperature rises. You can always remove a sweatshirt.
- Bring sunblock. The air temperature may be cool, but there is absolutely no protection from the sun out there in the high race track bleachers. Unless you're in a luxury box, without protection you're going to get burned.

- Bring a hat and sunglasses.
- Bring binoculars. On the larger tracks — Daytona, Talladega, Pocono — when the cars are on the opposite side of the track they look miniscule. Binoculars will help you scan the far side of the track, as well as the pits and garage areas.
- Bring a small transistor radio. As with most sports, the trackside announcements are barely heard at a raceway. But with a small radio and an earphone, you'll be able to dial into the local radio telecast provided by the Motor Racing Network or the Performance Racing Network and be able to hear the live play-by-play action.
- If you have a portable police scanner, bring it. During the race, drivers talk with their crew chiefs and their spotters who are located around the track. With a scanner you can eavesdrop on these conversations and get an inside look on race strategy. Be warned, in the heat of battle drivers may not use the best language.
- Buy earplugs. The noise level at a race track is incredible and exciting, but it's not all that healthy for young ears. If you're bringing along the kids, stop by any of the souvenir trailers. A pair of earplugs sells for about $1 or $2.
- Stopwatches are fun but not necessary. If you've got one, bring it along. You'll be able to track lap times and speeds to see which drivers are turning the fastest lap on the track. If you don't have one, don't despair. The play-by-play announcers will provide this information during the radio telecasts.

Ultimately, the goal is to pack lightly. You'll be doing a lot of walking and a heavy load will only increase the stress and strain. Food and drink can be bought at the track. While refreshments are usually overpriced — hey, they're trying to make a living, too — the extra cost sure beats lugging around a couple cans of soda and a bologna sandwich all day.

As far as souvenirs go, it's wise to wait until the end of the race to make your purchase. The trailers stay open for hours after the race and buying them before adds more to your load. (This suggestion goes out the window if you're bringing kids. Here you'll want to get something to keep them out of your hair during the race.)

And when the race is over, plan on spending a long time getting out of the track. It can take hours to get out of the parking lot, to then sit in traffic on the local interstate.

The First Race

The first Winston Cup race for any fan is a magical experience. The smells, the sounds and the fans combine for an amazing moment that can't be translated to the small screen at home. Simply put, you've got to be there.

But if you find yourself shut out of a Winston Cup event, don't worry, there are other ways to take in some major league, and some not-so-major league racing without the stress and strain.

If you live anywhere near a Winston Cup facility, check into the availability of tickets for the support race or for qualifying day. Usually, the events held on Saturday in advance of the Winston Cup event on Sunday, pack a lot of racing action at a reasonable price. Prices and availability vary track by track, although the tickets will cost just a sliver of what the Winston Cup entrance costs.

Pole day tickets for major events at most tracks go for between $5 and $10. The added benefit to either support race days or qualifying days is that those sessions are followed by practice by the Winston Cup starts. Moreover, those same drivers will often turn up behind the wheel in cars in the support race.

Good racing, however, isn't limited to Winston Cup. Every Saturday night at tracks across the country, local stock car drivers do battle for the fun of it. Saturday night racing allows fans to get an up close look at the sport without having to sit in traffic for hours and spend hundreds of dollars.

If you've got any reservations about the sport, going to a local short track first may be a wise decision. There, in addition to seeing good action, you'll get to meet some of the local drivers.

Local racing is not pretty. The cars aren't as sleek or fast as those on the Winston Cup circuit, but there is no better place to get a taste of the sport without the hassle. If you're unsure where a nearby facility may be located, check out the National Speedway Directory, which is issued annually and lists tracks by state.

Important Numbers

Airlines

American Airlines	(800) 433-7300
America West	(800) 235-9292
Continental	(800) 525-0280
Delta	(800) 221-1212
Northwest	(800) 225-2525
Southwest	(800) 435-9792
United	(800) 241-6522
US Airways	(800) 428-4322

National Hotel Chains

Adam's Mark Hotels	(800) 444-2326
Best Westerns	(800) 528-1234
Clarion Hotels	(800) 252-7466
Comfort Inns	(800) 228-5150
Courtyard by Marriott	(800) 321-2211
Days Inns	(800) 325-2525
Econo Lodges	(800) 446-6900
Fairfield Inns	(800) 228-2800
Friendship Inns	(800) 453-4511
Hampton Inns	(800) 426-7866
Hilton Hotels	(800) 445-8667

Holiday Inns	(800) 465-4329
Howard Johnsons	(800) 654-2000
Hyatt Hotels	(800) 233-1234
La Quinta Motor Inns	(800) 531-5900
Marriott Hotels	(800) 228-9290
Omni Hotels	(800) 843-6664
Quality Inns	(800) 228-5151
Radisson Hotels	(800) 333-3333
Ramada Inns	(800) 228-2828
Red Roof Inns	(800) 843-7663
Residence Inns	(800) 331-3131
Ritz-Carltons	(800) 241-3333
Sheraton Hotels	(800) 325-3535
Super 8 Motels	(800) 800-8000
Westin Hotels	(800) 228-3000
Wyndham Hotels	(800) 822-4200

Rental Cars

Alamo	(800) 327-9633
Avis	(800) 331-1212
Budget	(800) 527-0700
Dollar	(800) 421-6868
Enterprise	(800) 325-8007
Hertz	(800) 654-3131
National	(800) 328-4567
Thrifty	(800) 367-2277

14

TEAM SHOP ADDRESSES

Making Contact
with Your Favorites

Can't get to the track? Drop your favorite driver a note at the team shop. If you're looking to get a picture autographed, be sure to include a self-addressed, stamped envelope to make it easier for the driver to return your photo.

And if you're in the neighborhood of any of the shops, don't hesitate to stop in. Many of the larger teams offer shop tours and racing museums. If you're lucky, you might even bump into a driver while you're there.

Teams are listed by car numbers. Drivers listed were current as of March 1997. Drivers occasionally change teams; however, the car number stays with the team owner.

No. 1
Driver: Jerry Nadeau
Precision Products Racing
P.O. Box 569
Hwy 16 North
Denver, NC 28037
(704) 483-9340

No. 2
Driver: Rusty Wallace
Penske Racing South
136 Knob Hill Road
Mooresville, NC 28115
(704) 664-2300

No. 3 & 31
Drivers: Dale Earnhardt (3), Mike Skinner (31)
Richard Childress Racing
P.O. Box 1189
Industrial Drive
Welcome, NC 27374
(910) 731-3334

No. 4
Driver: Sterling Marlin
Morgan-McClure Motorsports
25139 Lee Hwy
Abingdon, VA 24211
(540) 628-3683

No. 5, 24, 25
Drivers: Terry Labonte (5), Jeff Gordon (24), Ricky Craven (25)
Hendrick Motorsports
P.O. Box 9
5315 Stowe Lane
Harrisburg, NC 28075
(704) 455-3400

No. 6 &16
Drivers: Mark Martin (6), Ted Musgrave (16)
Roush Racing
P.O. Box 1089
5835 Hwy 49 South
Liberty, NC 27298
(910) 622-5160

No. 7
Driver: Geoff Bodine
Geoff Bodine Racing
6007 Victory Lane
Harrisburg, NC 28075
(704) 455-1777

No. 8
Driver: Hut Stricklin
Stavola Brothers Racing
P.O. Box 339
2240 Highway 49 North
Harrisburg, NC 28075
(704) 455-6461

No. 9
Driver: Lake Speed
Melling Racing
2004 Pitts School Road
Concord, NC 28027
(704) 786-4635

No. 10
Driver: Ricky Rudd
Rudd Performance Motorsports
P.O. Box 6010
Mooresville, NC 28115
(704) 664-4372

No. 11
Driver: Brett Bodine
BDR Motorsports
304 Performance Road
Mooresville, NC 28115
(704) 664-1111

No. 15
Driver: Larry Pearson
Bud Moore Engineering
P.O. Box 2916
400 North Fairview Street
Spartenburg, SC 29034
(864) 585-8155

No. 17
Driver: Darrell Waltrip
Darrell Waltrip Motorsports
P.O. Box 293
6780 Hudspeth Road
Harrisburg, NC 28075
(704) 455-3117

No. 18
Driver: Bobby Labonte
Joe Gibbs Racing
9900 Twin Lakes Parkway
Charlotte, NC 28269
(704) 875-2895

No. 19
Driver: Gary Bradbury
TriStar Motorsports
103 Center Lane
Huntersville, NC 28078
(704) 948-8919

No. 21
Driver: Michael Waltrip
Wood Brothers Racing
Route 2, Box 77
636 Mayo Court
Stuart, VA 24171-9511
(540) 694-2121

No. 22
Driver: Ward Burton
Bill Davis Racing
301 Old Thomasville Road
High Point, NC 27260-8190
(910) 887-2222

No. 23
Driver: Jimmy Spencer
Travis Carter Enterprises
P.O. Box 540
3021 U.S. Hwy 421 South
Hamptonville, NC 27020
(910) 468-6896

No. 28 & 88
Drivers: Ernie Irvan (28), Dale Jarrett (88)
Robert Yates Racing
115 Dwelle Street
Charlotte, NC 28208
(704) 392-8184

No. 29
Driver: Jeff Green
Diamond Ridge Motorsports
5901 Orr Road
Charlotte, NC 28213
(704) 598-5295

No. 30
Driver: Johnny Benson
Bahari Racing
208 Rolling Hills Road
Mooresville, NC 28115
(704) 664-6670

No. 33
Driver: Ken Schrader
Andy Petree Racing
P.O. Box 325
East Flat Rock, NC 28726
(704) 698-0335

No. 36
Driver: Derrike Cope
MB2 Motorsports
185 McKensie Rd
Mooresville, NC 28115
(704) 664-7416

No. 37
Driver: Jeremy Mayfield
Kranefuss-Hass Racing
163 Rolling Hills Road
Mooresville, NC 28115
(704) 663-3700

No. 40, 42, 46
Drivers: Robby Gordon (40), Joe Nemechek (42), Wally
Dallenbach (46)
Team Sabco
114 Meadow Hill Circle
Mooresville, NC 28115
(704) 662-9642

No. 41
Driver: Steve Grissom
Larry Hedrick Motorsports
P.O. Box 511
Statesville, NC 28687
(704) 881-0410

No. 43
Driver: Bobby Hamilton
Petty Enterprises
311 Branson Mill Rd
Randleman, NC 27317
(910) 498-3745

No. 44
Driver: Kyle Petty
PE-II
7571 Flowe Store Rd
Concord, NC 28025
(704) 788-4400

No. 71
Driver: Dave Marcis
Marcis Auto Racing
P.O. Box 645
Skyland, NC 28776
(704) 684-7170

No. 75
Driver: Rick Mast
Buch Mock Motorsports
217 Rolling Hills Road
Mooresville, NC 28115
(704) 663-7572

No. 77
Driver: Morgan Shepherd
Jasper Motorsports
110 Knob Hill Road
Mooresville, NC 28115
(704) 662-6222

No. 78
Driver: Billy Standridge
Triad Motorsports
6006 Ballpark Rd
Thomasville, NC 27360
(910) 472-1482

No. 81
Driver: Kenny Wallace
Filmar Racing
2730 Zion Church Rd
Concord, NC 28025
(704) 786-8000

No. 90
Driver: Dick Trickle
Donlavey Racing
5011 Old Midlothian Pike
Richmond, VA 23224
(804) 233-8592

No. 91
Driver: Mike Wallace
Pro-Tech Motorsports
4372 Providence Mill Road
Maiden, NC 28650
(704) 428-4585

No. 94
Driver: Bill Elliott
Bill Elliott Racing
P.O. Box 456
Hickory, NC 28603
(704) 345-6102

No. 96
Driver: David Green
American Equipment Racing
7701-C N. Tyron St
Charlotte, NC 28262
(704) 510-0002

No. 97
Driver: Chad Little
Mark Rypien Motorsports
177 Knob Hill Road
Mooresville, NC 28115
(704) 664-8097

No. 98
Driver: John Andretti
Cale Yarborough Motorsports
9617 Dixie River Road
Charlotte, NC 28208
(704) 393-8579

No. 99
Driver: Jeff Burton
Roush Racing
122 Knob Hill Rd
Mooresville, NC 28115
(704) 664-3800

PUBLICATIONS

Staying on Top of the News

Suggested Reading

Magazines and Newspapers

Area Auto Racing News
P.O. Box 8547
Trenton, N.J. 08650
(609) 888-3618

Autoweek
1400 Woodbridge Ave
Detroit, MI 48207
(313) 446-6000

Circle Track Magazine
6420 Wilshire Blvd
Los Angeles, CA 90048-5515
(213) 782-2000

Inside NASCAR
The Quarton Group
888 W. Big Beaver
Suite 600
Troy, MI 48084
(810) 362-7400

NASCAR Winston Cup Scene
128 S. Tryon St.
Suite 2275
Charlotte, NC 28202
(800) 883-7323

NASCAR Winston Cup Illustrated
128 S. Tryon St.
Suite 2275
Charlotte, NC 28202
(800) 883-7323

National Speed Sport News
P.O. Box 1210
Harrisburg, NC 28075
(704) 455-2531

OnTrack
128 S. Tryon St.
Suite 2275
Charlotte, NC 28202
(704) 371-3966

Performance Racing News
593 Yonge St
Toronto, Ontario Canada M4YIZ4
(416) 922-7223

Racer Magazine
1371 E. Warner Ave
Suite E
Tustin, CA 92780
(714) 259-8240

Racing For Kids
P.O. Box 588
Concord, NC 28026-0588
(704) 786-7132

Speedway Scene
P.O. Box 300
North Easton, MA 02356
(508) 238-7016

Stock Car Racing Magazine
65 Parker St.
Suite 2
Newburyport, MA 01950
(508) 463-3787

Books:

Behind The Wall, A Season on The NASCAR Circuit, by Richard Huff. Bonus Books, 160 East Illinois St., Chicago, IL 60611.

American Zoom, by Peter Golenbock. Macmillan, 1633 Broadway, New York, NY 10019.

The Stock Car Racing Encyclopedia, by Peter Golenbock and Greg Fielden. Macmillan, 1633 Broadway, New York, N.Y. 10019.

Inside Track: A Photo Documentary of Stock Car Racing, by George Bennett and Benny Parsons. Artisian, 708 Broadway, New York, NY 10003-9555.

National Speedway Directory, by Allan Brown. P.O. Box 448, Comstock Park, MI 49321.

Supercars, The Story of The Dodge Charger and Plymouth SuperBird, by Frank Moriarty. Howell Press, Inc, 1147 River Road, Suite 2, Charlottesville, VA 22901.

Television Networks

ABC Sports
47 West 66th St.
New York, NY 10023

CBS Sports
51 West 52nd St.
New York, NY 10019

CNN Sports
One CNN Center
Atlanta, GA 30303

ESPN
ESPN Plaza
935 Middle St.
Bristol, CT 06010

The Nashville Network
2806 Opryland Dr.
Nashville, TN 37214

NBC Sports
30 Rockefeller Plaza
New York, NY 10112

TBS
One CNN Center
P.O. Box 105366
Atlanta, GA 30348

16

RACING STOCKS

Wall Street's Infatuation with Racing

While most fans aren't willing to sink four million dollars into the operation of a race team, it is possible for people today to have a financial stake, albeit minor, in companies heavily involved in motorsports.

In the past few years, a couple of major companies have gone public allowing people to buy stock in their operations. So far, the public offerings have been overwhelmingly successful.

Aside from the companies that own tracks, many of those that sponsor Winston Cup teams also sell stock to the public. Some of the sponsor stocks include the Exide Corporation, Lowes Home Centers, MBNA, Anheuser Busch, First Union and Sunoco.

Buying stock in these companies allows fans to have a partial ownership in the future of motorsports in this country. To get information on the financial performance of these companies call their investor relations departments and request an annual report. Also check with a local stock broker for information about making a purchase.

Here's a sample of the publicly traded companies involved with racing:

Dover Downs (DVD)
Owns Dover Downs International Raceway.

Grand Prix Association (GPLB)
Operates the Grand Prix of Long Beach, a track in Memphis and a track in St. Louis.

International Speedway Corporation (ISCA)
A subsidiary of NASCAR, owns Watkins Glen, Talladega, Daytona and Darlington.

Penske Motorsports (SPWY)
Owns Michigan, Nazareth, California Speedway and a piece of Rockingham.

Speedway Motorsports (TRK)
Owns Charlotte, Atlanta, Texas, Sears Point, Bristol and half of North Wilkesboro.

STATISTICS

Stock Car Racing Milestones

All-Time NASCAR Winston Cup Race Winners (1949–June 8, 1997)*

		# Wins
1	Richard Petty	200
2	David Pearson	105
3	Darrell Waltrip	84
	Bobby Allison	84
5	Cale Yarborough	83
6	Dale Earnhardt	70
7	Lee Petty	54
8	Ned Jarrett	50
	Junior Johnson	50
10	Herb Thomas	48
11	Rusty Wallace	47
12	Buck Baker	46
13	Tim Flock	40
	Bill Elliott	40
15	Bobby Isaac	37
16	Fireball Roberts	34
17	Rex White	28

		# Wins
18	Fred Lorenzen	26
19	Jim Paschal	25
	Jeff Gordon	25
21	Joe Weatherly	24
22	Benny Parsons	21
	Jack Smith	21
24	Speedy Thompson	20
	Mark Martin	20
26	Fonty Flock	19
	Buddy Baker	19
	Davey Allison	19
29	Harry Gant	18
	Neil Bonnett	18
	Curtis Turner	18
	Geoff Bodine	18
	Terry Labonte	18
	Ricky Rudd	18
35	Marvin Panch	17
36	Dick Hutcherson	14
	Lee Roy Yarbrough	14
	Ernie Irvan	14
39	Dick Rathmann	13
	Tim Richmond	13
41	Donnie Allison	10
	Dale Jarrett	10
43	Cotton Owens	9
	Paul Goldsmith	9
45	Jim Reed	8
	Kyle Petty	8
47	Bob Welborn	7
	A.J. Foyt	7
	Darel Dieringer	7
	Marshall Teague	7
51	Sterling Marlin	6
52	Alan Kulwicki	5

		# Wins
	Dave Marcis	5
	Ralph Moody	5
	Dan Gurney	5
56	Ken Schrader	4
	Hershel McGriff	4
	Billy Wade	4
	Glen Wood	4
	Charlie Glotzbach	4
	Bob Flock	4
	Lloyd Dane	4
	Eddie Gray	4
	Pete Hamilton	4
	Parnelli Jones	4
	Eddie Pagan	4
	Nelson Stacy	4
	Morgan Shepherd	4
	Bobby Labonte	4
70	Dick Linder	3
	Tiny Lund	3
	Bill Blair	3
	Frank Mundy	3
74	James Hylton	2
	Derrike Cope	2
	Elmo Langley	2
	Danny Letner	2
	Billy Myers	2
	Tom Pistone	2
	Marvin Porter	2
	Jimmy Pardue	2
	Gober Sosebee	2
	Gwyn Staley	2
	Emanuel Zervakis	2
	Johnny Beauchamp	2
	Al Keller	2
	Red Byron	2

		# Wins
	Ray Elder	2
	Bobby Johns	2
	Jimmy Spencer	2
91	Bobby Hillin, Jr.	1
	Lake Speed	1
	Phil Parsons	1
	Ron Bouchard	1
	Dick Brooks	1
	Jody Ridley	1
	Greg Sacks	1
	Lennie Pond	1
	Harold Kite	1
	Donald Thomas	1
	Johnny Allen	1
	Richard Brickhouse	1
	Bob Burdick	1
	Marvin Burke	1
	June Cleveland	1
	Neil Cole	1
	Jim Cook	1
	Bobby Courtright	1
	Mark Donohue	1
	Joe Eubanks	1
	Lou Figaro	1
	Jim Florian	1
	Larry Frank	1
	Danny Graves	1
	Jim Hurtubise	1
	Royce Hagerty	1
	Joe Lee Johnson	1
	John Kieper	1
	Paul Lewis	1
	Danny Weinberg	1
	Jack White	1
	Art Watts	1

	# Wins
Johnny Mantz	1
Sam McQuagg	1
Lloyd Moore	1
Norm Nelson	1
Bill Norton	1
Dick Passwater	1
Bill Rexford	1
Shorty Rollins	1
Jim Roper	1
Earl Ross	1
John Rostek	1
Johnny Rutherford	1
Leon Sales	1
Frankie Schneider	1
Wendell Scott	1
Buddy Shuman	1
John Soares Jr.	1
Chuck Stevenson	1
Tommy Thompson	1
Whitey Norman	1
Bobby Hamilton	1
Bill Amick	1
Mario Andretti	1
Earl Balmer	1
Brett Bodine	1
Ward Burton	1
Jeff Burton	1

149 Drivers

* These are the numbers according to NASCAR. There is some controversy concerning two wins recorded by Tiny Lund and one by Bobby Allison.

All-Time Team Owner Standings (1949–1996)

Owner	Entries	Wins	Earnings
Rick Hendrick	968	60	$35,596,702
Richard Childress	651	63	$27,499,852
Junior Johnson	1,071	139	$22,133,785
Jack Roush	450	18	$15,997,915
Robert Yates	271	27	$13,756,641
Harry Melling	390	34	$12,555,994
Bud Moore	911	63	$11,339,291
Petty Enterprises	2,009	269	$11,291,188
Wood Brothers	898	96	$10,643,227
Morgan-McClure	353	13	$ 9,411,434

Winston Cup Consecutive Years with Victories

Richard Petty	18	1960–1977
David Pearson	17	1964–1980
Darrell Waltrip	15	1975–1989
Dale Earnhardt	15	1982–1996
Ricky Rudd	15	1983–1997
Lee Petty	13	1949–1961
Cale Yarborough	13	1973–1985
Rusty Wallace	11	1986–1996
Bobby Allison	10	1966–1975
Bill Elliott	10	1983–1992
Terry Labonte	7	1983–1989
Davey Allison	7	1987–1993
Geoff Bodine	7	1988–1994
Mark Martin	7	1989–1995
Neil Bonnett	5	1979–1983
Harry Gant	4	1982–1985
Harry Gant	4	1989–1992
Buddy Baker	4	1970–1973

Kyle Petty	4	1990–1993
Dale Jarrett	4	1993–1996
AJ Foyt	3	1970–1972
Alan Kulwicki	3	1990–1992
Jeff Gordon	3	1994–1996
Sterling Marlin	3	1994–1996

NASCAR Winston Cup Champions (1949–1996)

1996	Terry Labonte
1995	Jeff Gordon
1994	Dale Earnhardt
1993	Dale Earnhardt
1992	Alan Kulwicki
1991	Dale Earnhardt
1990	Dale Earnhardt
1989	Rusty Wallace
1988	Bill Elliott
1987	Dale Earnhardt
1986	Dale Earnhardt
1985	Darrell Waltrip
1984	Terry Labonte
1983	Bobby Allison
1982	Darrell Waltrip
1981	Darrell Waltrip
1980	Dale Earnhardt
1979	Richard Petty
1978	Cale Yarborough
1977	Cale Yarborough
1976	Cale Yarborough
1975	Richard Petty
1974	Richard Petty
1973	Benny Parsons
1972	Richard Petty
1971	Richard Petty

1970	Bobby Isaac
1969	David Pearson
1968	David Pearson
1967	Richard Petty
1966	David Pearson
1965	Ned Jarrett
1964	Richard Petty
1963	Joe Weatherly
1962	Joe Weatherly
1961	Ned Jarrett
1960	Rex White
1959	Lee Petty
1958	Lee Petty
1957	Buck Baker
1956	Buck Baker
1955	Tim Flock
1954	Lee Petty
1953	Herb Thomas
1952	Tim Flock
1951	Herb Thomas
1950	Bill Rexford
1949	Red Byron

Multiple Winston Cup Championship Winners

7	Richard Petty	1979, 75, 74, 72, 71, 67, 64
7	Dale Earnhardt	1994, 93, 91, 90, 87, 86, 80
3	Darrell Waltrip	1985, 82, 81
3	Cale Yarborough	1978, 77, 76
3	David Pearson	1969, 68, 66
3	Lee Petty	1959, 58, 54
2	Terry Labonte	1996, 84
2	Ned Jarrett	1965, 61
2	Joe Weatherly	1963, 62
2	Buck Baker	1957, 56

2	Tim Flock	1955, 52
2	Herb Thomas	1953, 51

Rookie of The Year

1996	Johnny Benson
1995	Ricky Craven
1994	Jeff Burton
1993	Jeff Gordon
1992	Jimmy Hensley
1991	Bobby Hamilton
1990	Rob Moroso
1989	Dick Trickle
1988	Ken Bouchard
1987	Davey Allison
1986	Alan Kulwicki
1985	Ken Schrader
1984	Rusty Wallace
1983	Sterling Marlin
1982	Geoff Bodine
1981	Ron Bouchard
1980	Jody Ridley
1979	Dale Earnhardt
1978	Ronnie Thomas
1977	Ricky Rudd
1976	Skip Manning
1975	Bruce Hill
1974	Earl Ross
1973	Lennie Pond
1972	Larry Smith
1971	Walter Ballard
1970	Bill Dennis
1969	Dick Brooks
1968	Pete Hamilton
1967	Donnie Allison
1966	James Hylton

1965   Sam McQuagg
1964   Doug Cooper
1963   Billy Wade
1962   Tom Cox
1961   Woody Wilson
1960   David Pearson
1959   Richard Petty
1958   Shorty Rollins

Winston Cup Most Popular Driver (1952–1996)

1996   Bill Elliott
1995   Bill Elliott
1994   Bill Elliott
1993   Bill Elliott
1992   Bill Elliott
1991   Bill Elliott
1990   Darrell Waltrip
1989   Darrell Waltrip
1988   Bill Elliott
1987   Bill Elliott
1986   Bill Elliott
1985   Bill Elliott
1984   Bill Elliott
1983   Bobby Allison
1982   Bobby Allison
1981   Bobby Allison
1980   David Pearson
1979   David Pearson
1978   Richard Petty
1977   Richard Petty
1976   Richard Petty
1975   Richard Petty
1974   Richard Petty
1973   Bobby Allison

1972	Bobby Allison
1971	Bobby Allision
1970	Richard Petty
1969	Bobby Isaac
1968	Richard Petty
1967	Cale Yarborough
1966	Darel Dieringer
1965	Fred Lorenzen
1964	Richard Petty
1963	Fred Lorenzen
1962	Richard Petty
1961	Joe Weatherly
1960	Rex White
1959	Glen Wood
1958	Jack Smith
1957	Fireball Roberts
1956	Curtis Turner
1955	Tim Flock
1954	Lee Petty
1953	Lee Petty
1952	Lee Petty

NASCAR All-Time Money Winners — through 1996

	Driver	Starts	Winnings
1	Dale Earnhardt	542	$28,234,471
2	Bill Elliott	493	$16,256,985
3	Darrell Waltrip	689	$15,182,051
4	Terry Labonte	542	$14,485,403
5	Rusty Wallace	393	$14,420,035
6	Mark Martin	325	$11,920,208
7	Ricky Rudd	562	$11,526,339
8	Geoff Bodine	443	$10,444,550
9	Jeff Gordon	124	$10,326,804
10	Sterling Marlin	371	$ 8,940,657

	Driver	Starts	Winnings
11	Ken Schrader	359	$ 8,792,786
12	Harry Gant	474	$ 8,456,094
13	Dale Jarrett	290	$ 8,052,822
14	Kyle Petty	469	$ 7,876,740
15	Richard Petty	1185	$ 7,775,409
16	Morgan Shepherd	445	$ 7,401,249
17	Ernie Irvan	230	$ 7,337,309
18	Bobby Allison	717	$ 7,102,233
19	Davey Allison	191	$ 6,726,974
20	Michael Waltrip	330	$ 5,377,672
21	Brett Bodine	281	$ 5,124,505
22	Alan Kulwicki	207	$ 5,061,202
23	Dave Marcis	815	$ 5,050,459
24	Cale Yarborough	559	$ 5,003,716
25	Lake Speed	361	$ 4,184,592
26	Benny Parsons	526	$ 3,926,539
27	Rick Mast	216	$ 3,909,492
28	Ted Musgrave	184	$ 3,890,980
29	Neil Bonnett	362	$ 3,861,661
30	Bobby Labonte	125	$ 3,843,193
31	Derrike Cope	277	$ 3,740,318
32	Buddy Baker	698	$ 3,638,521
33	Jimmy Spencer	203	$ 3,571,592
34	Bobby Hillin	323	$ 3,359,125
35	Bobby Hamilton	168	$ 3,253,310
36	Hut Sticklin	225	$ 3,005,992
37	Dick Trickle	224	$ 2,897,295
38	David Pearson	574	$ 2,482,596
39	Tim Richmond	185	$ 2,310,018
40	Greg Sacks	239	$ 2,245,865

Modern Era First Time Winston Cup Winners — 1972–1996

1996	Bobby Hamilton
1995	Bobby Labonte
	Ward Burton
1994	Sterling Marlin
	Jeff Gordon
	Jimmy Spencer
1993	None
1992	None
1991	Dale Jarrett
1990	Derrike Cope
	Brett Bodine
	Ernie Irvan
1989	Mark Martin
1988	Lake Speed
	Phil Parsons
	Ken Schrader
	Alan Kulwicki
1987	Davey Allison
1986	Kyle Petty
	Rusty Wallace
	Bobby Hillin, Jr.
1985	Greg Sacks
1984	Geoff Bodine
1983	Ricky Rudd
	Bill Elliott
1982	Hary Gant
	Tim Richmond
1981	Morgan Shepherd
	Jody Ridley
	Ron Bouchard
1980	Terry Labonte
1979	Dale Earnhardt
1978	Lennie Pond

1977	Neil Bonnett
1976	None
1975	Darrell Waltrip
1974	Earl Ross
1973	Dick Brooks
	Mark Donohue
1972	None

Winston Cup Pole Winners — Modern Era (1972–June 8, 1997)

Drivers	Poles
Darrell Waltrip	59
David Pearson	56
Cale Yarborough	51
Bill Elliott	48
Bobby Allison	36
Geoff Bodine	35
Mark Martin	34
Buddy Baker	30
Terry Labonte	26
Alan Kulwicki	24
Richard Petty	23
Ricky Rudd	23
Dale Earnhardt	22
Neil Bonnett	20
Benny Parsons	19
Ken Schrader	18
Rusty Wallace	18
Harry Gant	17
Ernie Irvan	17
Rusty Wallace	17
Jeff Gordon	16
Davey Allison	14
Tim Richmond	14
Dave Marcis	12

Drivers	Poles
Donnie Allison	9
Bobby Isaac	9
Sterling Marlin	9
Kyle Petty	8
Bobby Labonte	8
Morgan Shepherd	7
Brett Bodine	5
A.J. Foyt	5
Ted Musgrave	5
Lennie Pond	5
Dale Jarrett	5
Loy Allen, Jr.	3
Ron Bouchard	3
Bobby Hamilton	3
Rick Mast	3
Joe Ruttman	3
Ward Burton	2
Ricky Craven	2
Greg Sacks	2
Michael Waltrip	2
John Andretti	2
Johnny Benson	1
Chuck Bown	1
Jeff Burton	1
George Follmer	1
Robby Gordon	1
Jimmy Hensley	1
Jermey Mayfield	1
J.D. McDuffie	1
Joe Millikan	1
Mike Skinner	1
Sam Sommers	1
Jimmy Spencer	1
Ramo Scott	1
Hut Sticklin	1

Drivers	Poles
Dick Trickle	1
Kenny Wallace	1
Rick Wilson	1

Top Ten 200 mph-plus Qualifiers

Driver	Qualifying Speed	Race
Bill Elliott	212.809	1987 Winston 500
Bill Elliott	212.229	1986 Winston 500
Bobby Allison	211.791	1987 Winston 500
Davey Allison	210.610	1987 Winston 500
Darrell Waltrip	210.471	1987 Winston 500
Bill Elliott	210.364	1987 Daytona 500
Dale Earnhardt	210.360	1987 Winston 500
Kyle Petty	210.346	1987 Winston 500
Sterling Marlin	210.194	1987 Winston 500
Terry Labonte	210.101	1987 Winston 500

58 drivers have run faster than 200 mph during their careers. Cale Yarborough ran better than 200 mph on 15 occasions to top the list.

18

GLOSSARY

Words to Race by

Apron — The lower, flat portion of the track used for exiting and entering the pits, as well as in emergency situations.

Bite — If a car is loose, a driver will ask to remove a round of bite during the race, which is an adjustment made during a pit stop to remove extra weight to the right rear wheel. It's done by sticking a wrench through a hole in the rear window, over the wheel. It's also called **wedge.**

Blister — A condition that exists when tires are overheated. The surface bubbles and peels off.

Brake fade — In short track events where drivers rely heavily on the brakes, temperatures within the system will soar. Under extreme conditions, the brake fluid will boil, creating air bubbles in the system and reducing the effectiveness of the brakes. Teams install several wide air hoses directed at the brake rotor and calipers in order to cool the brakes.

Busch Grand National — A racing series one level below Winston Cup, often used as a training ground for drivers before breaking into the top ranks.

Camber — The tilt of a tire. Tires that are slanted in on the top display a negative camber. Tilted outside at the top is a positive camber.

Collectibles — Trinkets bearing a team's name.

Compression ratio — This is the ratio comparing the volume of an engine cylinder to the combustion chamber. In a 14:1 ratio, the cylinder volume must be 14 times larger than the combustion chamber, which is the small curved area where the fuel and air are ignited.

Depth gauge — Every tire has small holes across the surface. Tire specialists can tell how much useable surface tread exists by inserting the tool into the holes.

Dialed in — Drivers use this term to describe a car which has the optimum setup for a given track.

Draft — At top speeds on the fastest tracks, two cars running nose-to-tail can move faster than one car running alone. The first car cuts through the wind and the second can move freely though the already turbulent air using less power than the lead car.

Dynamometer — A machine used for testing and measuring horsepower. All engines are run through the "dyno" before being put into the cars.

Equalized — Goodyear Eagles incorporate an outer tire and an inner liner on the same wheel. Under normal conditions, the inner liner should have a higher air pressure level than the outer tire. Inner liners allow drivers to continue around the track when the outer tire goes flat. If the air pressure in the inner liner and outer tire become the same, the tire will cause the car to vibrate.

Firesuit — A suit made of fire resistant material designed to protect drivers in instances of fire. First introduced into Winston Cup racing in the mid-'60s.

Flat spotted — During spins or crashes, drivers lock up the brakes while the car is moving. As a result, the section of the tire in contact with the racing surface is worn down, creating a flat portion of the tire. Driving after such an incident produces a vibration in the car.

Fuel cell — A 22-gallon flexible fuel tank built to withstand severe impacts is mandatory on all cars.

Groove — The portion of the track where the cars move fastest. Typically, the groove will change during the race as rubber from worn tires grounds into the surface.

Handling — How the car reacts to the track.

Horsepower (hp) — A unit for measuring the amount of power generated by an engine.

Inspection — NASCAR inspects each and every vehicle entered into competition several times during each race weekend. They are last inspected prior to heading out onto the race track on race day. The cars of the top finishers are reinspected following the race.

Line — The fastest way around the track.

Loose — When going through the turns, the rear of the car feels like it's going to break free and spin around.

Lug nut — Bolt used to hold the wheels onto the car.

Marbles — An area in the upper portion of the track where bits of rubber, gravel and other waste tends to accumulate. Drivers going into this area get the sensation that they're rolling over marbles.

Pace car — A car driven by a NASCAR inspector which is used to pace the field around the track before the race and during caution periods.

Pit — An area on pit road assigned to each team from where they will perform in-race repairs and service.

Pit stop — Routine in-race servicing including tire changes, refueling, chassis adjustment and refreshments for the driver done by a team of about 12 men, although only seven are allowed to go over the wall.

Plug check — After running a few laps during practice, a driver will turn off the engine while on the track and coast into the garage area. This will allow the engine builder to examine the spark plugs to determine whether all cylinders are functioning properly. If a driver were to keep the motor running and drive to the garage, the results of a plug check would not be as accurate.

Polesitter — The driver who has turned in the fastest time in pre-race qualifying starts first or on the pole.

Push — If a driver says the car is pushing, he's having a difficult time turning. The sensation is that it will head straight for the wall. Drivers also call this tight.

Qualifying — A lap or series of laps used to find the fastest car in the field. Usually held on Friday afternoon prior to race day. A second round of qualifying is held on Saturday.

Qualifying motor — Engine builders create a motor specifically for qualifying. It's built to create the most possible horsepower, which is usually done by pushing the stress limits of the motor. While the motor may perform well for qualifying and the first practice session, it's not built to withstand the strain of running 500 miles. Crews will remove the motor after qualifying.

Restrictor plate — A thin plate that sits between the carburetor and the intake manifold, which was introduced in 1988 to lower horsepower produced at the superspeedways. The plates reduce the amount of air and fuel entering the engine and cut about 300 hp.

Roll cage — A structure built from of 1 3/4-inch tubing built around the driver's compartment and designed to withstand the impact of a crash.

Roof flap — Thin panels of metal that are mounted into the roof that are designed to stop a car from going airborne when spinning at high speeds. The panels break the air flow that would normally lift the car in such spins.

Scales — Every team uses scales as part of their normal set up of the car. They'll use them to find the overall weight of the car, as well as the specific weight being carried by each wheel.

Scuffs — Tires that have been used before. Occasionally, if during practice the driver finds the car works better on used tires, the team will intentionally wear in or scuff a few sets of tires for race day.

Set up — By adjusting such items as shocks, springs, camber, sway bars and track bars, teams work to create a basic combination or set up for each track.

Spoiler — Pieces of metal which extend across the rear deck lid creating down force on the back end of the car. NASCAR mandates the angle of the spoiler for each track.

Spotter — Every team has one member positioned high in the grandstands who is in radio contact with the driver and the crew chief. The spotter will alert the driver to any on-track obstructions, accidents or debris during the race. He'll also tell the crew when the driver is entering pit road for service.

Stagger — Tires on the outside of the car have a longer distance to travel around the raceway than the inside tires. To make up the difference in travel, the circumference of the outside tires is slightly larger than the circumference of the inside tires. The difference between the two sizes is called stagger.

Stickers — Brand new tires, which still have the Goodyear stickers on the surface.

Stop-and-go — NASCAR may penalize a driver for going too fast in the pits or for driving over an air hose during a pit stop. Occasionally, the penalty is a stop-and-go, whereby the driver would pull into the pits, come to a full stop before a NASCAR official, and then drive on.

Team hauler — Massive tractor-trailer combinations used to deliver a team's equipment to the race track. The hauler will carry two complete cars — a primary and a back up — five engines and enough equipment to completely rebuild a car while at the track.

Tire temperature — Tire specialists measure the temperature at three points across a tire's surface. The results provide an indication of how a car is handling on the track.

Toe — If viewing a car from the front, toe would be the amount the tires point inward or outward. If the tires point inward toward each other that would be a toe-in problem. Toe-out would be the opposite.

Track bar — Winston Cup chassis allows a team to adjust the roll-center of the car, by adjusting up or down, a bar extending from the rear end to the chassis.

Wedge — By turning adjusting screws reachable by sticking a long wrench through the rear window, a crew member can alter the weight distribution to the opposite wheels. For example, by turning a screw over the right rear wheel, a team member can shift the weight to the left front.

Window net — A web of nylon that is affixed to the driver's side window. The net is designed to both block material from entering the driver's compartment and to restrain the driver during crashes.

Winston cup — NASCAR's premiere level, the equivalent of the Major Leagues in baseball.

NASCAR's Flag System

During an event, NASCAR officials notify drivers of current race conditions through a series of flags. Those flags are displayed by the series' starter, who stands on a platform mounted high above the start-finish line.

NASCAR officials in an operations booth — also called the tower — radio information to the starter on when to show various flags.

Here are brief descriptions of each flag.

Green — The green flag is used to start the race and to signal the drivers that the track is clear for racing. At the beginning of the race, the cars must maintain their starting positions until they've crossed the start-finish line. The driver on the pole position must lead the field to the start-finish line.

Yellow — This flag is used to alert drivers of an accident or other roadway hazard ahead. Once they've been given the yellow flag, drivers cannot advance their on-track positions and must travel at a reduced speed. Under virtually all instances, when the yellow flag is displayed, the field is under the control of the pace car. No driver can pass the pace car, without officially being told to do so by NASCAR.

Red — When the red flag is displayed, cars on the track must stop immediately. If possible, the field will come to the start finish line. The red flag is used under extreme emergency situations when the track is blocked by safety crews following an accident or when the race is stopped by rain. While the red flag is out, no work is allowed to be done to the cars, either those on the track or those already in the pits.

Blue with yellow stripe — This flag signals drivers that faster traffic is approaching. Once being given the flag, drivers should move over and yield to the faster cars.

Black — When shown the black flag a driver must return to the pits immediately and discuss the situation with a NASCAR official. Usually, the flag is displayed because of a suspected malfunction with the car, such as an oil leak or if the hood or rear deck lid has worked loose. A driver ignoring the black flag is subject to disqualification.

White — The white flag signifies the lead car is on its final lap.

Checkered — When the checkered flag is shown, the lead car has completed the required number of miles or laps and the race is officially over.

INDEX

A

ABC, 112, 114
Accord Speedway, xi
Allison, Bobby, 27
Atlanta Motor Speedway, 101, 103, 139

B

Bahari Racing, 25
Baker, Buddy, 36, 42, 44, 48, 53, 84
Benson, Johnny, 45, 46, 52, 53, 58, 70, 98, 102, 106
Bill Davis Racing, 42
Becker, Bill, 97, 106
Brasington, Harold, 7
Brawley, Robert, 10
Brickyard, 400, 102
Bristol Motor Speedway, 140
Bodine, Geoff, 48, 49, 52, 56, 58, 69

Booth, Clyde, 22-24, 25, 30, 31, 56, 71
Bonnett, Neil, 53, 125
Bown, Chuck, 107
Burton, Jeff, 107, 129

C

CBS, 9, 110, 112, 115, 118
California Speedway, 37, 141
Campbell, Sir Malcolm, 5, 6
Championship Auto Racing Teams, 18
Charlotte Motor Speedway, 141
Charlotte Observer, 73
Childress, Richard, 71
Craven, Ricky, 43, 48, 61, 68, 121-123, 131

D

Dallenbach, Wally, 61
Darlington Raceway, 142

Daytona Beach, 5, 6, 16, 91
Daytona, 500, 9, 31, 53, 68, 102,
    110, 114, 115, 143
Disney, 11
Dover Downs International
    Speedway, 10, 47, 144
DuPont, 95, 107

E

Earnhardt, Dale, 9, 15, 22, 43,
    44, 53, 55, 60, 65, 71, 86, 95,
    101, 122, 127, 137
Elliott, Bill, 68
ESPN, 9, 109-112, 115
ESPN2, 115
Exide Corporation, 107, 179

F

firesuits, 124
Flock, Tim, 7
Floyd, Thomas, 98, 108
Forbes magazine, 4, 10, 55
France, William Henry Getty, 5,
    8, 13, 16
France, William Clifton, 5, 8, 9,
    56
fuel cells, 125

G

Gant, Harry, 9
Gordon, Jeff, 11, 13, 43, 44, 51,
    54, 55, 61, 65, 68, 91, 92, 101,
    107, 121
Gordon, Robby, 61
Goodyear Tire & Rubber, 37-40,
    136, 137
Goodwrench Service, 95
Grant, Stu, 37-40, 136

H

Hall, David, 113
Hammond, Jeff, 30, 32, 35, 36,
    41, 42, 72, 75, 76, 77
helmets, 125
Hendrick, Rick, 18, 57
Hewitt, Doug, 30, 31, 70, 71
Hopkins, Ronnie, Jr., 23, 127,
    128, 130, 131

I

IndyCar, 4
Indy Racing League, 18
Indianapolis Motor Speedway,
    38, 102, 145
International Speedway
    Corporation, 114
Irvin, Ernie, 22, 48, 61, 66, 125

J

Jarrett, Dale, 22, 44, 50, 66, 91,
    108
Jarrett, Ned, 8, 15, 17, 19, 46, 110
Johnson, Junior, 46

K

Kellogg's Corn Flakes, 95, 107
Kenin, David, 114
Kulwicki, Alan, 57, 67, 92

L

Labonte, Terry, 61, 65, 68, 91, 92,
    107, 108
Latford, Bob, 91, 92
Laughlin, Mike, Jr., 124
Letterman, David, 11

Little, Chad, 22, 32, 33, 45, 52, 58, 97
Lorenzen, Fred, 8

M

Major League Baseball, 114
Marcis, Dave, 48, 69
Marlin, Sterling, 44
Martin, Mark, 57, 65, 100, 106-108, 121, 122, 129
Martinsville Speedway, 146
McReynolds, Larry, 60, 71, 86, 89
Mecca, Paul, 106
Michigan Speedway, 147
Musgrave, Ted, 129

N

National Association for Stock Car Automobile Racing (NASCAR), xi, 3-6, 8, 10-14, 16, 17, 19, 20-22, 24, 29, 30, 32, 36-38, 40, 41, 45, 56, 58, 59, 64, 66, 67, 68, 74, 87, 93, 97, 98, 106, 109, 110, 114, 117, 118, 124, 126, 128, 129, 131, 134
NASCAR Cafe, 13
NASCAR Craftsman Truck Series, 13
NASCAR Thunder, 13
National Basketball Association (NBA), 4, 98
National Championship Stock Car Circuit, 6
National Football League, 114
National Hockey League, 4, 114
Nelson, Gary, 42
Nemechek, Joe, 61
New Hampshire International Speedway, 11, 148

North Carolina Motor Speedway, 149
North Wilkesboro Speedway, 11

P

Parsons, Benny, 46, 51, 52, 109, 113
Pearson, David, 8
Penske Motorsports, 10
Pennzoil, 98, 108, 136
Petty, Richard, 7-9, 11, 130
Phoenix International Raceway, 150
Pierantoni, Dayne, 72, 73, 76
Pocono Raceway, 150
Poole, Mel, 49, 50
Puryear, Ron, 25-28

R

Restrictor plates, 25-27, 33
Richmond International Raceway, 151
R.J. Reynolds Co., 8, 96
Roberts, Glenn (Fireball), 126
Roberts, Tom, 106
roll cage, 126
roof flaps/roof rails, 129
Roush, Jack, 18, 100, 129
Rudd, Ricky, 52, 67, 69, 88, 95
Rypien, Mark, 22

S

Sabates, Felix, 61-65, 67, 68, 71
Sears Point Raceway, 152
seats/seat belts, 128
Schrader, Ken, 48
Schumacher, Michael, 55
Shepherd, Morgan, 43

Simpson, Bill, 123-126, 130, 131, 137
Simpson Race Products, 123
Speedvision, 113
Sponsors Report, The, 103, 107, 108
Stant, 106
Squier, Ken, 110, 111

T

Talladega Superspeedway, 121, 153
TBS, 113, 115
Texas Motor Speedway, 11, 37, 154
Tide, 95
The Nashville Network (TNN), 3, 84, 108, 110, 112, 114, 115
Turner, Curtis, 7
Trickle, Dick, 48
Triplett, Kevin, 18, 45

U

Unocal, 19, 41

V

Valentine, John, 133-137
Valvoline, 100, 107, 136

W

Wagenhauls, Fred, 105
Waltrip, Darrell, 9, 27, 30, 32, 39, 44, 52, 57, 61, 62, 63, 66, 68, 105
Waltrip, Michael, 84
Wallace, Rusty, 21, 36, 48, 55, 57, 65, 67, 77, 122, 123, 131
Watkins Glen International, 154
Warner Bros., 11
Wheeler, Patti, 113, 115, 116, 117, 119, 120
wind tunnel, 29, 30, 31
window nets, 130
Winston Cup, 4, 7, 8, 9, 11, 13, 14, 19, 25, 26, 36, 39, 45, 49, 51, 53-56, 58, 59, 65, 71-73, 75, 77, 79, 81, 97, 103, 109, 112, 117, 122, 124, 133-135, 137
Wood Brothers Racing, 84
World Sports Enterprises, 113, 116, 120

Y

Yates, Robert, 18, 22, 26, 27, 50, 62, 65-67, 69, 70, 134
Yarborough, Cale, 8, 9, 111